THE COMF
MONEY P

ABOUT LEGAL & GENERAL

The Legal & General Group, established in 1836, is one of the UK's leading financial services companies and one of the UK's top 50 FTSE quoted companies. Over 5.2 million people rely on us for life assurance, pensions, investments and savings plans.

As part of Legal & General's Community Involvement programme, to which we contribute some £2 million per year, we are keen to promote financial literacy and improve financial awareness through charitable projects. Legal & General is delighted to support Age Concern's publication, *The Complete Money Plan*, as part of this programme. We hope that it will prove to be a useful financial planning guide for those approaching retirement. The publication has been entirely managed and produced by Age Concern and the charity has had full editorial control over content.

For further information on Legal & General's Community Involvement programme, please refer to our Corporate Social Responsibility Report at www.legalandgeneral.com/csr

Legal & General Group Plc
Registered in England No 1417162
Registered Office: Temple Court
11 Queen Victoria Street
London EC4N 4TP

Supported by

THE COMPLETE MONEY PLAN

A STEP-BY-STEP GUIDE TO HELP YOUR MONEY
LAST A LIFETIME

PAUL LEWIS

BOOKS

© 2004 Age Concern England

Published by Age Concern England
1268 London Road
London SW16 4ER

First published 2004

Editor Ro Lyon
Production Vinnette Marshall
Designed and typeset by GreenGate Publishing Services, Tonbridge, Kent
Printed in Great Britain by Bell & Bain Ltd, Glasgow

A catalogue record for this book is available from the British Library.

ISBN 0-86242-399-6

CONTENTS

ABOUT THE AUTHOR

Paul Lewis is a freelance financial journalist who writes widely on tax, benefits, and personal finance. His work appears regularly in *The Daily Telegraph*, *Saga Magazine* and *Reader's Digest*. Paul also presents *Money Box* on BBC Radio 4.

INTRODUCTION

People in their 50s go through great changes. At 45, almost half have children living with them; at 55 that has fallen to 8 per cent. At 55, barely one in six is retired; by 60 that has risen to more than half. It can be a time when mortgages are paid, debts are less, savings mature, money is inherited. But it also can be an age when redundancy looms and health may begin to decline. It is a time for moving house, for divorce, for changing jobs, for looking ahead to retirement. At every stage there are financial decisions to be made.

In some ways, people in their 50s are in financial limbo. They do not have the advantages that come with age at 60 or 65 – no pension, no Pension Credit, no Winter Fuel Payment, no free or cheap travel, no tax breaks. But nor do they have the advantages of youth – a lifetime of work ahead of them and enough time to correct a mistake or try another course entirely. Work is hard to find and yet help from the State assumes that work will be sought and found. Disability creeps up on some people but the benefits for disabled people are a nightmare of complexity. Ageism is rife.

Financial guides for people who have not retired tend to concentrate on younger people – those with 20 or 30 years of working and saving ahead of them. The particular financial needs and products for the over 50s are seldom addressed, and often not well understood by a young sales force. The people in their 50s who are catered for tend to be those with money; the irony is that for some it is the richest time of life while for others it can be a time of joblessness and worry.

If you are hitting 50 – or already there – this book is for you. Whether financially good or financially bad, your 50s will certainly be financially different. This book combines benefits information, financial planning, rights at work, and choices that have to be made by people in their 50s – with and without money.

Any book about money has parts that are relevant to you and some that you think are not. But remember, no-one thinks redundancy or divorce or ill health or widowhood will ever happen to them – until it does. So although parts of this book may seem miles – or years – away from you, that may not always be so.

The book is in four main sections. Many people in their 50s come into some cash, so it starts with 'Putting Your Money to Work', which is a guide to saving and investing and, of course, pensions.

Next comes 'Managing your Money', including cutting your expenditure, because your 50s is not the time to waste money. Every penny saved now is tuppence for your retirement when you will need it more. Cutting down on the tax you pay, managing debt and streamlining your insurance cover are all included here, as is information about what to expect when looking for financial advice.

Then there is the money down the sofa. Perhaps literally, but certainly metaphorically, billions of pounds goes wasted in unclaimed assets, private and public, that languish to other people's benefit. The section on 'Boosting Income' looks also at what social security benefits may be available should you need them, and looks ahead to what State Pension you might expect. If you're thinking of striking out on your own and setting up your own business, what you have to do is explained here, and so is making the most of your home as a financial asset.

The book finishes with the exciting and frightening bits – lives change in our 50s. Health goes, opportunities come, work alters, relationships change, retirement looms. Plan for it and it will be a lot better.

PUTTING YOUR MONEY TO WORK

Your 50s can be a time when you have spare cash for the first time. You may get a lump sum from your job due to redundancy or early retirement. You may come into an inheritance. Your children may be off your hands – financially at least – and your mortgage paid off. That investment you started ten years ago may suddenly mature and give you a pleasant surprise. So your 50s can be a time of having a bit of spare money. You may not be well off, however. Redundancy or retirement can mean a big drop in income that a modest lump sum will not replace. But one thing is for sure: you do not have a working life ahead of you and money decisions have to be made bearing in mind that retirement may crop up – voluntarily or otherwise – in the not too distant future.

If you do find you have some new money, it is important to put it to work at once. If it's allowed to, money will do as little as possible.

In this section:

SAVING

- Internet banking
- Tax on savings
- Interest rates
- National Savings & Investments

INVESTING

- The pros and cons of investing
- Government stock (gilts)
- Corporate bonds
- Shares and the stock market
- ISAs
- Complicated investments
- Annuities

PENSIONS

- Tracing old pensions
- Occupational pensions
- Personal pensions
- Enhancing your pension
- Annuities
- Spreading retirement
- Pension release
- Starting another pension
- Small funds
- Pensions in peril
- Pension protection

ALTERNATIVES TO A PENSION

- ISAs
- Property

SAVING OR INVESTING?

There is an important distinction between saving money and investing it. When you save money it remains yours – you lend it to a bank or finance company and it pays you for the use of it. When you invest money you do more than lend it, you buy something with it, such as shares, property, units in a trust, bonds or some other financial product. The company you paid for the item will normally promise to return your money to you at some time in the future. But you have to be careful. How much will the company pay? Will it give all the money back to you at the end? Even if it says it will give it back, can you enforce that promise? Generally, any investment puts your money at some risk. Risk means just what it says – there is a chance you will not get back what you paid out; indeed you may not get back anything at all.

Some things that are called 'investments' are really savings – for example, some products sold by banks and building societies that pay a guaranteed amount after a fixed number of years are sometimes called 'investments'. But on the definition used in this book, they are not. They are savings.

So the first thing to decide is whether to keep your money as short-term savings, or use those savings to buy an investment. It is a big decision. The best thing to do if you suddenly find yourself with some money is to keep it in cash for a few weeks or months until you have thought carefully what to do with it.

There are great advantages to money which is kept in a bank or building society account:

■ It remains your money. You do not buy anything with it; legally it is yours.

- It is safe. Banks and building societies almost never collapse in the UK and, even if one did, they all belong to a compensation scheme which protects most of your money up to £33,000 (see page 129 for details of compensation). If you are really worried and you have a lot more than that, then keep it in accounts with several banks or building societies. The limit applies separately to each company.

- It earns interest. Nowadays you can earn reasonable interest rates – especially if you use internet banking and especially if you pay basic-rate tax or less on your income.

- It is accessible. You can take it back to spend at any time. With some accounts you may lose some of the interest it has earned unless you give a certain amount of notice, but that is less common now than it used to be. There are also fixed term savings products with banks or building societies (they are sometimes called 'investments') where you cannot get your money back until the end of, say, two or five years.

The one big disadvantage with cash is that your money does not grow very fast. If you use the interest it earns as income, then inflation will eat away at its value. There are different ways to measure inflation, but using the traditional Retail Prices Index (RPI), prices have risen on average by 3.6 per cent a year over the last 20 years. Over that time, prices have roughly doubled and therefore the buying power of your money has roughly halved. If you had £1,000 in 1984 you would need around £2,000 now to buy as much. So if you put your money in a savings account, although you will get out the same amount in cash at the end plus whatever interest it has earned, it may be worth less.

The Government is now using a different index to measure inflation. It is called the Consumer Prices Index (CPI) and at the moment it gives a much lower rate of inflation than the RPI – around half. Over a longer period, however, the difference is less. In the 15 years from

November 1988 to November 2003 the RPI showed prices going up by two thirds, whereas the CPI showed them growing by about half. Which is the 'better' way to measure price rises is a matter for debate. But there is no doubt that the CPI – which is used throughout Europe and elsewhere – will come to be the standard way used by Government, pension providers and employers. Whatever measure we use, however, cash in the bank can buy less when we take it out than when we put it in many years before.

Nevertheless, the best place for any money you suddenly come into is a cash savings account with a bank or building society. Get it in there as soon as you can and then think about what to do with it in the long term.

SAVING

INTERNET BANKING

While your money is in a savings account you might as well put it to work. You can earn more money on your savings, have more control over your money at any hour of the day or night, and pay less for loans and overdrafts if you bank over the Internet.

Despite security fears in the early days, internet accounts appear to be as completely safe and secure as any other account. You will need an up-to-date computer to handle the security features they use. Of course, you also have to have an internet connection – preferably through broadband, which will speed things up.

If you look at the best buy tables for savings rates or interest on a current account, the top accounts will nearly always be on the Internet. The banks spend less on running them: you do not pay for branches and the staff that sit in them. Usually you do not get a

5

statement posted to you – you are sent an email when it is ready and it is up to you to download it or print it out. The banks are also trying to move customers to this cheaper way of banking, so they offer you good deals.

Internet accounts also put you much more in charge of your money. You can look at your account, move money around, check your balance, and see what payments have come in and gone out 24 hours a day 365 days a year. If you have any queries about your account or want to change the way you pay bills, you can do it all over the computer, although almost all of them have a telephone helpline as well if you get stuck. Some internet banks do not let you have a chequebook, so all payments have to be done electronically through the computer.

Nearly as convenient and offering excellent rates of interest, is the Internet's older cousin – telephone banking. Pick a bank with truly 24 hour 365 day coverage and you can check your balance, move money, make payments, and order documents at any time. So if you do not have a computer or cheap internet access, use the phone.

Despite the control you have over your money over the Internet or on the phone, many people are disappointed at the speed it takes to move money from one bank to the other. The money disappears from your account as soon as you press the return key on your keyboard or give your instructions on the phone, but it does not arrive in the recipient's account any quicker than it did when men in bowler hats walked round the City with bundles of cheques. Officially this 'clearing cycle' takes three working days, but it is often more. The day ends around 4pm, so instructions given after that count as the next day. Weekends and Bank Holidays do not count: for some reason money cannot travel on these days. Even when the money finally does arrive at the other bank, it may not appear in the recipient's account for another day or two after that.

While the money appears to trundle round the system, the two banks hang onto it. First one and then the other actually has the money and they invest it on what is called the 'overnight money market'. So they profit from the delays: no wonder that they say there is 'no demand' to speed things up. Things may change in 2005, however. New computer systems will allow same-day transfers as a matter of routine; but the banks may charge us for this privilege.

There is one exception to these snail-like movements of money. If you transfer funds from one account to another with the same bank – even if it is someone else's account – the money normally moves instantly. The moment it leaves your account it is in theirs. So it can be done.

> Although internet banking is safe, you still have to be careful and sensible. Never write down or store the details of your account on your computer or on anything that might be stolen. Also, there are crooks out there who send out emails by the million pretending to be from your bank and asking you to send them your security details by email or via a website. Your bank will never ask for information in this way and such messages should always be ignored. Treat these messages the same as you would a person who stood by a cash machine who told you they were from the bank and asked you to confirm your PIN. Ignore them.

Nevertheless, once you have taken the plunge with internet or telephone banking, you will never look back. Just look at the difference it can make. With an internet or phone savings account you can easily earn 4 per cent on your money – the top rate is currently 4.5 per cent. With a branch-based account you will be lucky to get more than around 2.5 per cent unless you put up with restrictions or have a high income.

TAX ON SAVINGS

Any interest you earn is normally taxed. Unless you tell the bank or building society that you are not a taxpayer, it will automatically deduct tax at 20 per cent off your interest. So that means even 4 per cent is worth just 3.2 per cent once you get it – and as little as 2.4 per cent if you pay higher-rate tax.

You will pay no tax if your total income in the tax year is less than £4,745 in 2004–2005. You will pay tax at the lower rate of 10 per cent if your income is less than £6,765 and you will pay higher-rate tax if your total income in the tax year is £36,145 or more.

If you are liable to pay tax, there are two ways to avoid it on your savings. First, you can put the money into what is called a 'cash ISA'. (ISA stands for Individual Savings Account). The interest on money in an ISA is always tax-free. The simplest and safest sort of ISA is just a savings account with the ISA name to protect it from tax – that way you can save your money in an account that pays the interest tax free. (Stocks and shares ISAs are explained on page 23.) You can only put up to £3,000 a year into a cash ISA (sometimes called a mini-cash ISA). That limit is due to be cut to £1,000 in April 2006. You can take the money out at any time, but you cannot put it back if that will mean you have put in more than £3,000 in the tax year. Cash ISAs are good news and everyone should have one. Even if you are just saving up for Christmas or a holiday, a tax-free cash ISA is a good place to do it. You can open a new cash ISA each tax year and you can transfer money in one ISA into another if you find a better interest rate. Check for penalties before you do, however.

Secondly, if you have a spouse who does not pay tax – or who pays it at a lower rate than you do – you can put the money in their name.

However, remember that this only works if you give them the money absolutely – it becomes theirs, not yours. So only do it if you are both comfortable with that and you have considered the implications of death, divorce, and bankruptcy.

INTEREST RATES

Most savings accounts have a variable rate of interest which will rise and fall as interest rates in general go up and down. You can get a fixed or guaranteed rate for a fixed period instead if that will suit your needs. For example, you may want to save up your lump sum until you reach 60 or 65, or until a child is 21 and you may have to help with a deposit for a house. The advantages are that you do know exactly what your money will earn over the fixed period, and that fixed rates are often slightly higher than the rates on other accounts. However, you will have to tie up your money for a time – the longer you commit to, the better the rate – and you will need at least £1,000 and usually more to get the best rates. If interest rates rise considerably, you may find yourself stuck with a poor return. Many banks and building societies offer fixed rate products, which are usually called 'term accounts' or 'fixed rate bonds'. But beware the word 'bond' as many investments, some of them very risky, use it. So if you want a safe investment of this sort, make sure it is a 'fixed rate bond'.

NATIONAL SAVINGS & INVESTMENTS

You cannot get much safer than the UK Government when it comes to saving your money. Everything with National Savings & Investments is backed by the State. You can get a variety of products, some of which pay out tax free. The returns are relatively low but there is no tax to pay so they are good for taxpayers, especially those who pay at the higher rate. Other products pay the interest gross; tax is due if you are a taxpayer. If you are not, then it is handy to get the interest paid gross automatically without having to register. They may also suit people who pay tax through self-assessment, putting off the moment when tax is due.

Despite its name, products from National Savings & Investments are best described as 'savings' rather than 'investments'. They carry no risk and the money remains yours, although there are restrictions with some of them as to when you can get it back.

Savings certificates offer tax-free capital growth over a fixed period of two or five years. There are stiff penalties for cashing in early. The rate of interest is not great, but for higher-rate taxpayers they may be good value. Index-linked certificates pay interest at a fixed amount above the rate of inflation. They are attractive if you think inflation is going to rise. The minimum amount you can pay into each certificate is £100 and the maximum is £10,000.

Capital and fixed rate bonds are similar and pay taxable interest gross each year. They last one, three or five years, and can give reasonable value. The minimum amount payable is £500 and the maximum is £1 million in total. Again, there are hefty penalties for cashing in early.

Income and pensioner bonds pay a regular monthly income at a fixed rate for one, two or five years. The best rates are given to people aged 60 or more. Interest on both is taxable, but income bonds have the tax deducted, while pensioner bonds do not. The minimum and maximum amounts are the same as for capital and fixed rate bonds, and they too bring tough penalties for cashing in early.

Premium bonds are popular with higher-rate taxpayers. Interest at 2.6 per cent is put into the prize fund and you have one chance in 27,500 of winning in each monthly draw. Prizes are tax free and there is always that small chance of winning £1 million. The minimum amount is £100 and the maximum is £30,000. If you buy the maximum you have a good chance of winning a prize every month.

Guaranteed equity bonds grow for five years at a proportion of the growth in the FTSE 100 index of shares in our biggest hundred companies. If the index falls over that period then you get your original investment back in full. The bonds are not always available. Unlike other bonds related to the stock market, they are safe because they are backed by the Government; they are essentially a sort of savings with a rather complex way of working out the interest that will be paid. The return is paid gross and is taxable in the year it is paid.

All National Savings & Investments products are explained on its website (www.nsandi.com) and through its helpline on 0845 964 5000.

INVESTING

Before you think about investing the money for the long term, look at your overall financial position. In particular, do you have debts? If you do, it will normally be better to use your spare money to pay that debt off. You will never make more by investing £1,000 than the money you are being charged to borrow it. So pay off your credit card debt, get rid of the overdraft and see if you can pay off any bank loans early without being charged heavy penalties. (There is more about debt in the section starting on page 84.) Even paying off the mortgage may be a better deal than investing money. Once you have paid off your debts, you will have more free income and you could then start thinking about investing that if you want to.

After you have put your money in a high interest account for a while and paid off your debts, you need to think what you are going to do with it. Of course, you can leave it there earning interest and growing slowly. There is nothing wrong with doing that. However, almost all financial advisers and people who have been involved with saving and investing for many years will tell you that to make more than the 4 per cent your money earns in a good savings account you must invest it. Investment is different from saving. It means giving your money to someone else to use in the hope they can make it grow fast enough for them and you to see the advantage. In one sense you are buying an asset – such as a bond or a share – but those assets are only worth what someone else will pay for them in the future.

THE PROS AND CONS OF INVESTING

Before you decide what to do with your money, you should ask certain key questions:

- **Risk** Is your capital safe? If not, what is the worst that could happen? What has happened in the past? Is the same thing likely to happen in the future? Why?
- **Return** Does the scheme produce income or capital growth? If it provides income, is it guaranteed? How is that achieved? How often is the income paid? If it provides capital growth, how long can that continue? Always remember to take account of inflation and tax.
- **Access** Is your money tied up? If so, how long for? What is the notice period before you can cash in your investments? Are there any limits on the amount you can take out? What is the cost of

taking your money out? Is there a penalty for early withdrawal?
Are there costs of buying and selling to take into account?

- **Charges** How much is the investment going to cost, whether it
  performs well or not? How much upfront? How much each year?
  What do you get for those charges? How much will the charges
  reduce the investment returns?

- **Protection** Are you dealing with a reputable and authorised
  firm? Is it regulated? If it is not based in the UK, who regulates it?
  How much of your money is protected by a compensation
  scheme if the company goes bust?

- **Taxation** Is the scheme right for you from a tax point of view?
  If you are a non-taxpayer, are the returns paid gross without tax
  deducted? Will the income from the scheme mean that you pay
  a higher rate of tax? What happens to your investment when
  you die?

Some investments are safe. They are called fixed interest investments
and they can be with the Government or National Savings &
Investments or a building society. They will give you a guaranteed
return each year, and at the end of the period of the investment they
guarantee to give back the money you invested. Returns on these
investments can be slightly higher than a savings account and the
rates are fixed and guaranteed. You pay for that in the inflexibility;
your money is normally locked up for a few years while the
investment lasts. With some, you can withdraw money early if you
pay a penalty. With others, the capital cannot be recovered until the
end of the period. With government stock, you can sell it but you
may get less than you paid for it.

Most advisers who talk about investments, however, actually mean
gambling your money on the long-term growth in companies – either
by buying shares or, for a more cautious approach, buying 'bonds' in
a company. There are two reasons they do that. The first reason is

that, over the last 100 years, money which has been invested in shares has grown faster than money kept in cash or in fixed interest investments. If the past is a guide to the future, then over a long period of time, investment in stock market based products will be a better way to wealth than saving. The second reason is that advisers make their money, or some of it, out of the commission paid on financial products. The best commissions are normally paid on investments linked to the stock market; many fixed interest products pay no commission at all.

However, there are problems with stock market based investments that are often not made clear by the people who promote and sell them:

- **Your money is at risk** Shares can indeed go down as well as up. They can even plummet, as they did in the early years of this century. Although you can minimise this risk, all stock market based investments can result in your getting back less money than you put in. That is especially true if you cannot control the time when you need to cash your investment in. You may need the money to pay a debt, to invest when you retire, or to help a child with a new home; but that moment may be just the worst time to cash in a stock market investment.

- **Your money is unavailable** To get your money back you have to sell the investment and pay two sets of costs. First there is the 'spread', which is the investment term for the mark-up every vendor makes. If you bought a car from a dealer for £5,000 you would not expect to get £5,000 if you sold it the next day to another dealer. It is the same with shares. The selling price is always more than the buying price. With investments the spread is generally quite small – around 1 per cent in many cases, although if you are buying shares in small companies it may be much more (up to 10 per cent). Second, you cannot sell shares yourself: you have to go through a broker and they will charge you for their work. That charge may either be a flat fee of between around £10 to £25, or a percentage of perhaps around ¼ per cent.

■ **Time is against you** Stock market investments generally perform best over the long term – that can mean as long as 20 years according to the Financial Services Authority, and 25 years is probably the minimum safe time to be as sure as you can be that your shares will have grown in value. People in their 50s may not have that long to wait. There have been many periods of 5, 10 or 15 years when shares have been worth less at the end than they were at the start. So when you need the money – to retire, pay off a debt, fund your children through university, pay a tax bill – may be the wrong time to sell. Of course, if you need the money, you have to sell.

■ **Not all your money will be invested** In the first year as much as 6 per cent of your money can be taken as an upfront fee; in other words, you invest £100 and only £94 is used to buy shares. Nowadays these upfront fees are getting lower and may be zero, but it is always worth asking. Generally, the riskier the investment the higher the fee.

■ **Money will disappear every year** The company looking after your fund will take an annual fee. Typically that will be around 1½ per cent, although some investment funds will charge more (up to 2½ per cent). Some will charge less than this, but charges will seldom be less than 1 per cent. Part of this money is used to pay commission to your adviser – called trail or renewal commission – every single year that the investment continues. You can avoid this annual charge by investing in shares yourself, but other charges then come into play. Picking your own shares and investing directly in them is best avoided by beginners.

The advice in this book is cautious. It assumes that you do not want to return to your money in five years and find that half of it has gone. This section briefly lists different places to invest – as opposed to save – your money. It starts with the safest and moves on to riskier ways to invest. Advisers will tell you that risk leads to reward; but, remember, if it always led to that it would not be a risk. Risk means that your capital, or some of it, may disappear.

GOVERNMENT STOCK (GILTS)

Gilts are probably the safest form of pure investment. When you buy a gilt you lend money to the Government which guarantees to pay you a fixed rate of interest for a fixed period of time and then give you all your money back. The interest is taxable and is normally paid gross in two instalments each year.

You buy gilts on the market, either directly from the Government's Debt Management Office or through brokers. Either way there will be some small charges to pay. Overall, the return you get on a gilt is in many ways the fairest rate of interest you can get. It is in effect fixed each day by the financial markets at what is seen as a fair return over the period of the gilt. Although gilts run for a fixed period, you can sell them at any time, although you may get back less than you paid.

The prices of gilts are listed each day in the *Financial Times*. You can buy and sell gilts by post on a form available at post offices or from the Bank of England on 0800 818614. You can find out more about gilts on the Debt Management Office website at www.dmo.gov.uk

---

You can also invest in other 'sovereign' bonds, which can be with foreign governments or institutions like the World Bank or International

Monetary Fund. As they are backed by governments, they are all low risk, or at least as low risk as that particular government.

CORPORATE BONDS

Companies also issue fixed rate bonds, similar to gilts, but without the security of government backing. A corporate bond is a loan to a company in exchange for which it gives you a fixed and guaranteed rate of interest and a promise to give you back your capital at the end of a fixed period. The risk is that the company will go bust or be unable to honour the bonds it has issued. Bonds are rated from AAA through A and B to BBB. The better the rating the lower the return – because there is less risk you will not get your money back. However, even some AAA rated companies have gone bust. So you must remember that – even though most advisers will tell you they are lower risk than investing in shares – corporate bonds are not risk free. Once you get below AA, the risk is probably not worth taking. BBB bonds are known as 'junk' bonds; they do carry a high risk of default, but pay 3 or 4 per cent above AAA bonds.

SHARES AND THE STOCK MARKET

When most people talk of investment they mean putting your money into shares. A share is simply a very small part, often a billionth or less, of a whole company. When you buy shares in a company you make your money in two ways:

- The company pays out some of the profit it makes among the shareholders. This is called a 'dividend'.
- The price of the shares rises, so you can sell them for more than you paid for them.

So the investment is intimately linked to the performance of that company. If it makes strong profits, you will get dividends and other people will want to buy the shares, so the price will go up. If the company loses money, dividends will dry up and the price of shares in it will fall. If it goes bust, then you will lose everything. It is that simple – and that risky.

The other risk is simply timing. Even if shares in a company, or all the shares you own, generally speaking rise in value over time, the exact price you will get on a particular day may not be a true reflection of what that share is worth. Timing is against you in your 50s. As you move through this decade you have less time to wait for the market to improve and you should consider moving your money out of risky investments into more certain ones.

Buying shares

Shares are bought and sold on the stock market. The price of shares over the long term does depend on rational factors – the company's profits, the management team, its plans for the future, the business it is in. But the price also depends on intangible things like 'sentiment' and 'confidence'. In particular, the price of a share may rise because people in the market believe demand for it will rise. It will be worth more tomorrow, so they buy it today to make money. (It is worth noting that although investors are always told to invest in shares for the long term, the value of those shares is largely determined by very short-term variations as the people who really make – and lose – money on the stock market buy and sell minute by minute.) That happened in 1998 and 1999 when people believed that shares in technology companies and those based generally around the Internet could only rise in value. As a result the price did rise, even though many of the companies had no financial plans that showed them ever making a profit. Then in early 2000 the bubble burst and the great sell-off began, companies went under, and shares trading for tens of pounds were reduced in price to pennies. Many people lost a lot of money, and the stock market as a whole fell for the next three years. So for those who had to take their pension or use an investment to pay off a mortgage as share prices plunged, the timing was as bad as it could be.

Collective investments

The financial services industry has spent much of the last 50 years constructing complex structures around the simple principle of shares. These fulfil two functions – they protect you from some of the risk; and they provide a good income for the industry whether share prices rise or fall.

The most basic structure is the 'fund'. Instead of putting your money into one company or choosing your own selection of shares, you buy a 'unit' in a fund which invests widely across many types of share. As some shares fall, others will rise, and overall it is hoped that the fund will grow. These are usually called 'collective investments' and there are several sorts:

- The most common and probably the simplest is a **unit trust**. It is a fund which invests in the stock market and, when you buy a share of that fund, your money is spread across all the investments in the unit trust. Your share is represented by a number of 'units' in the trust which you can buy and sell as you want.
- Growing in popularity are **investment trusts**. They are actually companies which invest in the shares of other companies. Your investment is a share in this holding company. They can borrow money and are freer to take risks than unit trusts and the value of

shares in them is likely to go up and down by larger amounts. They are not regulated by the Financial Services Authority (FSA).

- **Open Ended Investment Companies (OEICs)** are a sort of combination of unit trusts and investment trusts. They are a much more common way of investing in other countries and they are regulated by the FSA. For those reasons some advisers think that they will eventually replace unit and investment trusts.

Whichever sort of collective investment you choose, you have to choose between two ways for your money to be invested:

Trackers

Trackers or passive funds simply invest the money in a representative sample of all companies traded on a particular market. You can buy a UK tracker or a Japan tracker, a Far East tracker or one that follows high-tech companies or big ones. The idea is that as the overall value of shares in this type of fund grows, your money will grow with it. Trackers are hitched to a particular stock market index; usually geographic, such as London or Tokyo, but sometimes a technology index.

Trackers do not always perform well. Of course, when markets fall, so does your money. If you are investing for the long term that should not matter. Over the very long term, stock markets generally rise in value and so will your money. But some do not follow the markets very efficiently, and, of course, the fund charges you for the cost of investing your money and to pay the adviser who sold you the investment. These charges are partly offset by reinvesting the dividends the shares earn.

Managed funds

Managed or active funds are run by an investment manager backed up by a team of researchers. They buy and sell shares in companies according to their view of what is going to do well. Sometimes they will take your money out of the stock market altogether and put it in cash or property. Some funds allow you to make some of these decisions. For example, some confine themselves to Asia or the USA; others specialise in smaller companies or ones in property or precious metals.

These experts watch everything that is going on and use their skill and judgement to invest your money to get the best return. Sadly, most of them do less well than money invested in trackers. Of course, each year some funds will do much better. Some – a very few – will do better year after year. However, the research shows that picking the fund that will do well next year and in the future is impossible. There is no 'persistency' as it is called. That is why there are now strict controls by the Financial Services Authority on the 'past performance' figures that can be used in adverts. The FSA's own research found past performance is generally not a good predictor of future performance. The one exception is that bad performance does tend to persist; but good performance does not. So choosing a fund on the basis of how it did last year or in the last five years is not necessarily going to produce a good return in the future.

The other big disadvantage with managed funds is that they cost a lot more to run and you pay for that through the annual charges. Whereas a tracker will charge you around 1 per cent a year – some a bit more, some a bit less – a managed fund may charge you 2 or 2.5 per cent a year and sometimes charge you an upfront fee as well.

Ethical

You can also find funds that invest what is called 'ethically'; in other words, they avoid putting money into companies trading in things such as armaments, drugs, farming, gambling, tobacco, alcohol, pornography, or nuclear power. You can choose a fund that fits your own ethical profile. There is conflicting evidence about whether these funds perform better or worse than conventional managed funds.

The FTSE index of shares in London includes an index of so-called ethical companies (FTSE4Good). There are UK, European and US versions of this index. You can find out more on the FTSE website at www.ftse.com/ftse4good/index.jsp

Safer

A fund does not have to invest in shares of companies listed on the stock market. It can invest in gilts, in corporate bonds, or in a mixture. It depends entirely on your attitude to risk and where you want your money.

With profits

You can also put your money in what is called 'with profits' investments. That misleading term is used for a collective investment run by an insurance company and invested partly in shares, partly in property, partly in cash, partly in bonds and other things. With profits investment only works if:

- you trust the insurance company completely; and
- you do not want to understand what is going on.

Nowadays, neither of those things is true for most people. Many experts expect that these problems combined with tougher regulation will be the death of with profits over the next decade.

ISAs

Individual Savings Accounts (ISAs) are not an investment (nor indeed as their name suggests 'savings') but a way of saving or investing which the Government allows to be tax free. You can put almost any investment into an ISA – or to be more precise you can find and buy almost any investment that has the ISA wrapping around it. When they were launched in 1999 all investment and growth in an ISA was tax free, but that is no longer the case.

There are two sorts of ISA to think about – **cash ISAs** are the most popular and were explained on page 8.

Stocks and shares ISAs (or equity ISAs) is the misleading term used for the other sort of ISA. Here the money is not saved: it is invested, but not always in stocks and shares. The returns on ISAs invested in shares are not tax free. Basic-rate tax is deducted from the dividends earned by the shares and since April 2004 is not refundable. So you effectively pay basic-rate tax on the money earned by your stocks and shares ISA. The three million people who pay higher-rate tax do better because they are exempt from paying any higher-rate tax on the ISA. The 100,000 people who pay Capital Gains Tax also benefit because no CGT is due on the gains the ISA makes.

The best way round this, apart from taking out a cash ISA, is to choose an ISA where the money is not invested in shares but is in corporate bonds, gilts, securities, or some other fixed interest investment. The returns on those are completely free of all tax, including basic-rate tax.

You can invest up to £3,000 in a stocks and shares ISA in each tax year (if you do not have a cash ISA you can invest £7,000 in one).

COMPLICATED INVESTMENTS

Avoid any investment that seems to use complicated methods you do not understand to give you a return well above the normal returns that are available. Most of the financial scandals of the last few years have centred round products that seemed too good to be true. They were. If you do not understand it, do not invest in it. It may cost you a fortune.

ANNUITIES

One way to convert a lump sum into an income for life without worrying about where it is invested is to buy an annuity. You give a lump sum to an insurance company and it gives you a guaranteed income for life. They are called 'purchased life annuities' and are almost identical to the annuities you buy with your pension fund (see pages 37–40). They are taxed differently, however.

All the income from a pension fund annuity is taxable. That is because the contributions you pay into a pension are free of tax, so the Treasury takes the tax when the income is generated. A purchased life annuity is different. You buy it out of your taxed income. So part of the money you get each month is treated simply as a return of your capital and is not taxed. Only the extra money – the interest your money is earning – is counted as income and is taxed. How much is taxed depends on your age and sex – the older you are, the more of your money is tax free.

You have to make the same choices as you do with a pension annuity about whether you want the income to rise with inflation; a guaranteed period to protect your heirs if you should die early; and/or a joint or single-life annuity. (There is more about these choices on pages 39–40. Similarly, in your 50s the amount you will get is very little – there are examples of this on pages 183–184.)

PENSIONS

TRACING OLD PENSIONS

People change jobs, employers move or change their names, and people forget about small contributions paid into personal pensions. So it is very important to check that there are no missing pension funds that could boost your income. Details of around 200,000 schemes are held by the official Pension Schemes Registry (see address on page 241) which runs a free tracing service for people who have lost touch with an old occupational or personal pension.

The more information you can give, the better the chance of tracking down your pension. They will need the name and address of any employer who might have run a scheme you belonged to. Information about that employer, such as whether it was part of a largor group or if it traded under any other names, will be helpful. It is also useful to be clear about tho typo of ponoion ochcmc you belonged to, was it an occupational pension scheme, a personal pension scheme or a group personal pension? Dates when you joined and left, or worked for the company (which may not be the same thing) will also help. If you are trying to find a personal pension, the name of the insurance company it was with or the adviser who sold it to you will be important.

You can get the form by calling 0191 225 6316 or fill it in online at www.opra.gov.uk/traceAPension

If the Pension Schemes Registry cannot track down the pension, you could try the Unclaimed Assets Register (see pages 136–137), which will charge you £35 for tracing an old pension.

It may be that you do not have a pension entitlement from an old scheme. Your employer may not have run a scheme, or you may have chosen not to join it. Even if you did, you may have had your contributions refunded when you left the company. Until 1975, you could get all your contributions back. From April 1988, you could get a refund of contributions if you had paid in for less than five years. After that the period was reduced to two years. It is possible that you did that but you have now forgotten. It is also possible that your pension rights were transferred to a new employer or to a personal pension.

If all else fails you can get help from the Pensions Advisory Service (OPAS). It can help with all pension enquiries including pensions with your employer, personal pensions, stakeholder pensions or even state pensions. Call OPAS on 0845 601 2923 or look at its helpful website at www.opas.org.uk

OCCUPATIONAL PENSIONS

Many people pay into a pension scheme operated by their employer. But many of us do not really know what the scheme promises or if those promises will be kept.

There are two sorts of pension scheme operated by employers. These pensions are called 'occupational' schemes because they are run as part of your job or occupation; but are sometimes called 'company' schemes (although not all of us work for a 'company') or 'employer-run schemes'.

Salary-related schemes

Salary-related schemes promise you a pension which is a certain percentage of your salary. With some schemes you get a sixtieth of your pay for each year you have paid into the scheme. So after 30 years in the scheme you get $\frac{30}{60}$ths or half your salary. You will also be able to have up to 1½ times your salary as a tax-free lump sum, but you will pay for that with a lower pension, so in practice most schemes offer eightieths of your pay rather than sixtieths. In the public sector in particular, you will get a pension of eightieths of your pay and a lump sum of $\frac{3}{80}$ths for each year you are in the scheme. In the past, the salary which was used to calculate your pension was normally the best of the last three years' salary before you retired or left the scheme. These schemes were normally known as 'final salary' schemes. However, to cut costs, a new variation is to base the pension on your average salary over all the years you are in the scheme. The averaging takes account of inflation but in many cases will provide a lower pension than a final salary scheme, although for some people they will be better. They are usually called 'career average' salary schemes.

These schemes also normally provide:

- **life insurance** of up to four times your pay if you die in service;
- **a pension for your widow or widower** or other financial dependent (typically of half your pension, although some offer two thirds); and
- **inflation proofing** of up to a maximum of 5 per cent a year for the pension earned from 1997 to 2004, and up to 2.5 per cent for pension rights earned from April 2005. Pension earned before 1997 may not be inflation proofed at all. In public sector jobs, pensions are increased each year in line with the Retail Prices Index.

Salary-related schemes are often called 'defined benefit' (DB) schemes because the amount of the pension – the benefit – is defined. In the past, they were often called 'superannuation'.

Money purchase schemes

Money purchase schemes simply save up all the contributions made into your pension by you and your employer into a pension fund. The money in the fund is invested, mainly in shares in most cases, and a certain portion of that fund belongs to you in proportion to the amount you and your employer have paid in. When you retire, your share of that fund is available to buy you a pension. You can choose to take some of it – usually up to a quarter – as a tax-free lump sum to do what you like with. The rest has to be used to buy a pension which will last the rest of your life – that is done through what is called an 'annuity'. (There is more information on annuities on pages 37–40.) The income you get from the annuity will depend on how much the money invested in the fund has grown, current long-term interest rates, and your age. There are normally no guarantees.

These schemes are also known as 'defined contribution' (DC) schemes, because it is the amount you pay in which is fixed, not the pension you get at the end.

Other kinds of pension schemes – personal pensions, group personal pensions, stakeholder pensions, self-invested personal pensions (SIPPs) – are all money purchase schemes. When you retire, you get a pension fund which is your money back, any tax relief that has been paid in, and any investment returns – minus, of course, the charges made for running it. You must use at least three quarters of that fund to buy a pension.

Some employer's schemes will be contracted out of the State Earnings-Related Pension Scheme (SERPS), which is now known as State Second Pension. That means you will pay less in National Insurance contributions. Salary-related schemes are almost all contracted out, but many money purchase schemes are not. (There is more about contracting out on pages 154–156.)

Increasing your pension

In every employer's scheme you are offered the chance to pay extra into your pension. There are different ways to do that:

Added years

Added years may be available if you are in a salary-related scheme, especially in the public sector or in some large well-established company scheme. You can pay extra money to buy 'extra years' in the scheme. So if you joined ten years ago, you may be given the chance to pay some extra money and be counted as if you have been in the scheme for 12 years for example. That may boost your pension by $\frac{2}{60}$ths of your salary when you retire. Generally, extra years are the best way to boost your pension because money paid now buys you a pension related to your salary and you can take a bigger lump sum. You can usually arrange to pay for the added years either as a lump sum or as a bigger deduction from your pay.

Additional Voluntary Contributions (AVCs)

AVCs can be paid on top of any pension that you or your employer pays into. At the moment, employees cannot pay more than 15 per cent of their annual pay into a pension. Hardly any scheme requires employee contributions anywhere near as high as 15 per cent. So AVCs to top up your contributions to closer to 15 per cent can seem a good idea. However, there are four reasons why they may not be:

- If you are in a final salary scheme, AVCs do not buy you more pension in that scheme. Instead, they are simply a separate money purchase scheme.
- Charges for AVCs can be high and they may not offer good value for money.

- You cannot take any of the fund as a lump sum – all of it has to be converted into a pension. This rule does not apply if you have been paying in since before 1987, and it will be changed from April 2006.
- You may be better off paying into a stakeholder pension.

There are two sorts of AVC. Every company scheme must offer you a choice of AVCs which you can join and pay in contributions through your pay; in other words, the contributions come straight off your money before you see it. These are normally called 'in-house' or 'in-scheme' AVCs. Your employer will have done a deal with the choice of AVC providers and charges will normally be low.

You can also pay into AVCs through a pension plan run entirely separately from your company scheme. These are called Free Standing AVCs (FSAVCs). You have to arrange to make the payments into FSAVCs yourself. Charges for FSAVCs are normally higher than those for AVCs and most advisers do not recommend them. If you are paying into an FSAVC scheme, consider stopping it and paying the money instead into in-house AVCs or a stakeholder pension. You may also have a claim for mis-selling if a financial adviser persuaded you to buy an FSAVC instead of an AVC from your company scheme (see pages 127–129 for details of how to complain).

Stakeholder pensions

Stakeholder pensions are also money purchase schemes. But they have several advantages over AVCs:

- Charges are lower – a maximum of 1 per cent a year of your fund can be taken as a management charge. Some schemes charge less than this. The lower the charges, the less they will drain away from your fund and, other things being equal, the faster your money will grow.

- When you retire you can take up to 25 per cent of your stakeholder fund as a lump sum; with AVCs you cannot do that.
- You can put up to £3,600 a year into a stakeholder pension without worrying about the 15 per cent limit on contributions. The limit of £3,600 will be scrapped with other pension reforms in 2006.

At the moment, employees who pay into a company scheme can only pay into a stakeholder pension as well if they earn less than £30,000 a year and are not a company director.

Since October 2001 employers with more than four staff which do not have an occupational scheme have had to offer their employees a stakeholder scheme. This change was meant to boost the amount paid into pensions, but it has failed to have the impact the Government hoped. Almost all employers have fulfilled their legal obligations and started a scheme, but three quarters of those schemes have no members at all – in other words, the scheme is there, but no employee has joined.

One big reason for this lack of interest is that employers do not have to contribute to the scheme themselves, so there is really no incentive for the employees to pay in. With more traditional occupational schemes the employer makes a contribution as well. It is much harder to build up a decent pension if your employer does not pay in too.

The other problem is that the employer may not choose the best stakeholder scheme. Employees may get lower charges and a scheme with a better investment record by finding their own stakeholder pension and paying into that.

PERSONAL PENSIONS

If there is no pension at your workplace, you may have paid into a
personal pension or its predecessor, the 'retirement annuity contract'
or Section 226 (s.226) pension. Nowadays, they are more likely to be
called stakeholder pensions, but essentially they are all the same –
money purchase schemes.

At the moment there are complex limits on how much you can put
into a money purchase pension scheme. The Government will sweep
all these rules away in April 2006 and replace them with a much
simpler regime. There will be a maximum increase in the value of the
fund of £215,000 in any one year, with people able to contribute up
to 100 per cent of pay or £3,600 (whichever is the larger), and a
lifetime limit on the pension fund value of £1.5 million. That may seem
a lot of money but a fund of that size would currently buy an inflation-
proofed pension for a man of 65 of around £75,500 a year – or
around £56,500 if he took his maximum lump sum. This maximum
will also apply to final salary schemes – they will be limited to
providing a pension of £75,000 a year.

Those upper limits will not affect most people, although people in their
50s will benefit from the flexibility of being able to put in a large
amount in one year – if they get a lump-sum payment, for example.
For most of us the problem is getting enough in our pension fund to
provide a pension we can live on. In January 2004 some sobering
figures were published by the Economic Affairs Committee of the
House of Lords. These showed the percentage of their salary that men
and women had to save to give them a pension of two thirds of their
pay on retirement – the sort of pension that final salary schemes offer.

How much you need to save depends on when you start – if you
start at 25 you have more time to pay in and your money has longer

to build up. Estimates produced for the House of Lords Committee showed that a man who started saving for his pension at 35 needed to save 24 per cent of his pay each year until he was 65 to have a reasonable chance of a pension worth two thirds of his salary. A woman needs to save more – 27 per cent. Women live longer and need a bigger fund to provide their pension for more years.

Contributions into a pension scheme as percentage of salary to give a pension of two thirds salary at 65

Starting age	25	35	45	55
Contribution rate (%)				
men	17	24	37	72
women	19	27	42	84

Assumptions: (1) earnings will rise 2 per cent a year above inflation

(2) investments will grow at 3 per cent a year above inflation

Most people, of course, do not save this much – usually far less. Even people in occupational pension schemes save less than that. The average contribution by employers per member in money purchase schemes is just 6.8 per cent, and their employees pay in 3.4 per cent. Even in private sector final salary schemes the contributions are only 12 per cent by employers and 4.9 per cent by employees. That is one reason why the funds which are there to pay final salary schemes operated by private companies in the UK have around £100 billion too little in them to meet their promises.

People who have put off saving for a pension until their 50s, or even their late 40s, face an almost impossible task. But whatever your pension it is important to find out what you can expect. If you pay into a final salary scheme then the scheme itself should be able to tell you what you are entitled to now and what you will be entitled to if you work until 60 or 65 or beyond. Remember that early retirement can have a very debilitating effect on a final salary scheme. Your final salary – or your career average pay – will be less, and the percentage of it you are paid as a pension will also be less. This double whammy can have a surprising effect. For example, if you retire at 50 on a salary of £30,000 after 20 years' service, then your pension, at 1/60th a year, would be £10,000. But if you work another five years and get promotion and pay rises to £40,000, then your pension at 1/60th a year would be £16,667 a year. That is a big boost for your pension for an extra five years' work. Your 50s are the ideal time to ask your company about the choices you have and the pension you can expect retiring at 60, 65 or even 70. Remember to factor in expected promotions and pay rises.

In some salary-related schemes, especially in the public sector, your employer may be willing to enhance your pension in exchange for early retirement if that suits them. These deals are much rarer than they used to be, however.

ENHANCING YOUR PENSION

People paying into money purchase schemes either through work, or through a personal or stakeholder pension, face a more difficult task. The first thing to do is to check what pensions you have been paying into. It is easy to lose track as you change jobs. The Pension Schemes Registry (see page 25) can put you in touch with schemes you may have belonged to in the past but lost touch with.

Once you have tracked down any old pensions, then you will want to know what they might be worth when you retire. There are four factors which will affect that:

■ How big is the fund now?
■ What age do you intend to retire?

- How big will your fund be then?
- What pension will that fund buy you?

How big is the fund now?

The first question is easy – your pension fund provider will tell you how big the fund is now. If it is an old pension you have not been contributing to for some years, it may be disappointingly small. The pension provider will continue to take charges from the fund – these will be at least 1 per cent a year and could be more. These charges act as a constant drag on any growth in the fund due to investment. Secondly, of course, the stock market fell for more than three years. From the start of 2000 to March 2003 the value of shares on the London Stock Exchange fell by more than half. Although the market recovered in the last nine months of 2003, at the start of 2004 it is still – at the time of writing – about the same level as it was in 1997. So share investments over that six-year period will not show any growth even before charges.

When will you retire?

The later you retire, the better, as far as your pension is concerned of course. The fund has more time to grow and any pension has to be paid for less time. If you are in an occupational scheme, it will have rules about the age you can retire and draw your pension. If you are in a personal or stakeholder pension, you can retire and draw your pension at any age from 50 to 75, although the lower age will be raised to 55 by 2010. However, if you are paying into an old personal pension you began before 1 July 1988 – called a retirement annuity contract or a Section 228 pension – you cannot retire and draw it until you are 60. Retiring before that is generally not a good idea anyway. Apart from the fact that your pension will be less and will have to cover you for more years of retirement, some have penalties built in. You should check your contract and ask your pension provider.

How big will your fund be then?

No-one knows how big your fund will be; and if they did they would not be allowed to tell you. When a financial services company predicts what your pension fund may be worth it has to use standard assumptions about the growth in investments. These assumptions are set down by the Financial Services Authority. Since 1999 the FSA has set down three rates of growth that can be used for pensions. They are 5 per cent, 7 per cent and 9 per cent a year. Despite a review in 2003 – when growth rates had been negative for nearly three years – the FSA stuck by these predictions. That means that any pension provider will show you what your pension fund might be worth in the future by assuming growth at one or more of these rates. After that the company will deduct its own charges and give you a figure, or a set of figures, to cover all three options. The only exception is if the company believes these growth rates are too high for the investment mix it uses – in which case it has to use lower ones.

It is important to realise that these figures are not guaranteed. They are illustrations and use growth rates laid down by the FSA. The company does not stand behind these rates of growth – still less guarantee them.

It is a sobering thought that shares on the London Stock Exchange have shown no growth in a quarter of all the ten-year periods over the last century. So the terrible truth is that no-one has the slightest idea how big your pension fund will be when you retire at some date in the future.

Once you have retired, you generally have to take your fund and convert it to a pension. So if your pension age is at a time when the stock market is low, your fund can be much less than you expect. Between January 2000 and March 2003 the value of shares on the London Stock Exchange fell by more than 50 per cent, potentially halving the value of the pension fund which someone retiring in March 2003 may have been expecting.

Some funds – but not all by any means – do allow you to protect your fund as you approach retirement by moving the money out of risky investments like shares into more stable investments such as government bonds or cash. This is sometimes called 'lifestyling'. It can be a good idea as it reduces the nasty surprises in store for you. In your 50s, it is a good idea to ask your pension fund if it is possible to do this. Some schemes, especially stakeholders, do it automatically. It is a complex area, so get advice.

What pension will your fund buy?

Normally a pension fund has to be converted into a pension when you retire. Sometimes you may have specified a retirement age when you took the pension out. Some companies will make you honour that date by imposing financial penalties if you retire earlier or later; in other words, they will keep some of your fund as a punishment. When you do decide to 'retire' or at least to take your pension, it normally has to be converted into a pension for life (an annuity).

ANNUITIES

Annuities are basically a bet between you and the insurance company. You give it a lump sum and it promises you an income for life. It estimates how long you will live and works out how much your declining fund will make over those years. It then builds in its profit and a margin for error and pays you a pension so that on average, when you die, your fund will be exactly exhausted. If you live an average time or less than average, the insurance company wins the bet. If you live much longer than average, the insurance company loses the bet.

Over the last 15 years the value of the annuity you can buy with a given fund has fallen by almost half. There are three reasons for that. The first reason is that life expectancy continues to grow – and people who take out annuities tend to live longer than other people. The second reason is that the returns on investments have been falling. Since 2000 the stock market has failed to live up to the heady promises of the 1990s, and interest rates on safer investments have declined sharply. So a longer life has to be supported by a fund that is now expected to yield lower returns. The third reason is that insurance companies have got these two key predictions of life expectancy and investment returns wrong in the past, so they build in a bigger margin of error than they used to. To win the bet you thus have to live a lot longer than average.

Because these calculations are complex and depend on predictions, insurance companies come up with different answers. For some reason most people still accept the figures given by the company that provided their pension. But everyone has the right to choose any annuity provider: it is called the 'open market option'. By choosing the right annuity provider rather than one of the worst, you can boost your income by 30 per cent.

There is a major problem with the open market option, however. Although customers are free to choose where they buy an annuity, insurers are under no obligation to sell them one. If you have £100,000 then you can pick from the whole market. But many big insurers set a lower limit on the funds they will accept; many set a lower limit of £10,000 for accepting funds saved up with a rival. So for people with small pension pots, there is often little or no choice – they have to go with the company they saved up with, and if it offers a bad deal, there is little they can do. Even a financial adviser may be reluctant to help. With a small fund there is little commission for them in trying to find the best deal, so they will not normally take the job on; but if you already have an independent financial adviser they may be more helpful.

New rules which start in April 2006 will allow you to take small funds as a lump sum. You can do this only once. But it applies to any number of funds which in total are less than the limit. That is set at 1 per cent of the maximum lifetime value of a pension, so will start at £15,000 (see page 32).

Which type of annuity?

When you come to choose an annuity you will be faced with several choices;

Flat or rising – a flat annuity will be fixed for life and so after 20 years of inflation will be worth far less than at the start. A rising annuity will keep up with inflation – measured by the Retail Prices Index – or you can choose for it to rise at 3 per cent or 5 per cent each year. Of course, it will start off far lower. At 55 the best annuity for a man with a pension fund of £100,000 which keeps up with inflation is £3,857 a year at time of writing. One that never rises will begin at £5,952, nearly £2,100 more and boosting your initial income by 54 per cent. That may seem attractive at 55 but may not seem too clever when you reach 85 and your pension is worth much less. Buying an annuity at 55 is not generally a good idea anyway.

Guaranteed or not – do you want the annuity to pay out for a guaranteed period even if you die meanwhile? The money could go to your heirs, thus avoiding the natural sense of injustice if you have just handed over £100,000 of your pension fund and you die within a year. The cost of this protection is negligible (less than £5 a year to guarantee the pension for five years), so if you have heirs you may want to consider it.

One life or two – if you are married or live with a partner, you can ensure that the annuity continues to be paid to them if you die first. You can choose for the whole of the pension to go to them, or a half or two thirds. This choice will, of course, reduce the income from your annuity while you are alive; by around 15 per cent for a man of 55. As women normally live longer, however, it will have little effect for them, and a joint annuity can be a good deal for a woman; or at least for her partner. Every couple should consider this choice carefully – it would clearly be wrong for a man to choose a higher pension now and leave his widow destitute. The Equal Opportunities Commission would like a law to force partners to get joint signatures on single life annuities to make sure that the matter has been discussed and agreed between them.

Impaired life – if you have a disease which could shorten your life, then you will get a higher income from an annuity. Being a regular smoker of ten cigarettes a day or more can also enhance the annuity income (by around 8 per cent).

A traditional annuity is fixed for life – you know how much it will be from the moment you buy it to the day you die. Falling interest rates have led some insurance companies to offer a 'variable annuity', the amount of which is related to a fund which is invested. These annuities can go up and down as the fund does better or worse. Some are linked completely to the stock market, and these have proved a disaster for some people. Others are invested in safe, fixed interest investments. The choice is yours, but there are risks involved.

When should you retire?

You can draw a personal pension as late as 75 and as early as 50 – although that will be raised to 55 by 2010 under government plans. So one major decision in your 50s is when to retire. The general rule is – don't do it in your 50s if you can help it, but if you must, the later the better.

A man of 50 with a pension fund of £100,000 can buy an index-linked pension for life of only £3,432 a year, and most people's funds are a lot less than that. If he hangs on for five years, it goes up by just over £400 a year. If he hangs on until he is 60, it goes up by £1,000 a year and another £1,000 if he can wait until he is 65. So instead of £3,432 at 50, by 65 he will get £5,395 for the same money; and, of course, if he is still in work he will have paid in for another 15 years so his fund should be rather bigger too.

You have more choice if you have several pensions – as many people now do. In that case you could consider drawing one if you need some money now and leaving others until later.

SPREADING RETIREMENT

The income from an annuity seems very low to most people. There are now two alternatives to buying one:

Income drawdown

With income drawdown you defer buying an annuity until you are 75. Strictly speaking this method is called 'income withdrawal option' but is generally called 'drawdown'. It is usually a bad idea.

With drawdown, you take the maximum tax-free lump sum (usually a quarter of the fund), and the balance of your pension fund is moved to a drawdown plan. That is invested and is very much like a pension fund. Each year you take out a sum of money to live on; the amount is set down by the Inland Revenue. The maximum is roughly equal to what you would get if the fund was used to buy a good annuity. You can take less than the maximum but there is also a minimum, which is 35 per cent of the maximum. The limits are reviewed every three years and so your income may change at that time. Because the fund is still invested, and because all these changes take work, charges and commission are taken from your fund each year.

The advantages of drawdown are:

- If you die, the amount in the drawdown fund can be inherited, less a 35 per cent tax charge.
- You can choose to buy an annuity later when market conditions may be better.

The big disadvantages are:

- No-one knows when or if annuity rates will rise – they may fall further. Under current laws, you will have to buy an annuity at 75 anyway.
- Charges are being taken off your money in retirement – once you have bought an annuity no more charges are deducted.

Even the people who sell them say that no-one should consider drawdown unless they have a fund worth at least £250,000.

Phased retirement

An alternative to drawdown for those with a personal pension is phased retirement. You divide your pension fund into chunks – as if it was a series of smaller funds – and then draw on each chunk separately.

When you 'retire', for that particular chunk you can take the 25 per cent lump sum and use the rest of the chunk to buy an annuity. The other chunks remain in the pension fund until you choose to use them.

The risk you take is that annuity rates will fall and you will get less for the chunks you use later. The advantage is that you can leave your pension fund to a spouse or other beneficiaries free of tax.

Both drawdown and phased retirement will seem good if annuity rates rise, but are bad or disastrous if they stay the same or fall. Timing the market, as the professionals call it, is difficult at best, impossible at worst. For people in their 50s it is almost always better not to retire at all. More flexible ways of drawing money from your fund will begin from April 2006.

Statutory Money Purchase Illustration (SMPI)

Just as Santa has his elves, somewhere in the bowels of Government or regulator there is a team of people who dream up incomprehensible names for simple things. Every year your pension provider has to tell you what your pension might be worth when you reach the age to sit back and think 'why didn't I save more?'.

In a neighbouring room sit another team to convert the incomprehensible names into shorter but even less meaningful acronyms. Please welcome the Statutory Money Purchase Illustration – or SMPI for short. Almost everyone who has a pension which is not a salary-related one has to be given a SMPI once a year. It is supposed to answer the simple and not unreasonable question 'what will my pension be worth when I retire?'.

In the past, pension providers have given us very large numbers in answer to that question but have conveniently forgotten to take account of the effects of inflation. £1,000 in 2004 will buy barely half what £1,000 would buy in 1984. A pension of £50,000 a year in 2020 may sound a lot but by then £50,000 may be barely enough to scrape along on. The new SMPI has to take account of inflation when it predicts the value of pensions. It does this by telling us what the pension will be worth in today's money.

The pension forecast in a SMPI is a lot smaller than the illustrations we have seen before. That is supposed to scare people into saving more. Or it may just make us all give up entirely.

Although better than previous attempts, the figures given are still pure fiction. They assume investments will grow by 7 per cent a year and inflation will be 2.5 per cent a year. No-one knows if either of those figures will be true. They never have both been true at the same time and the chances are they won't be in the future.

If you have a Section 226 retirement annuity contract from before 1 July 1988 you do not have to be given a SMPI, but your provider probably will send you one anyway.

PENSION RELEASE

It is always a bad idea to accept the blandishments of companies that invite you to 'release your pension'. Converting your pension into cash in your 50s is always a bad idea. You will see adverts for such schemes on daytime television, and in the press, inviting you to release or unlock your pension. They target people in their 50s who have a personal pension or one or more defined contribution schemes from past employments. They know that people in their 50s who have lost their job or taken early redundancy, or whose marriage has broken up, can be short of cash. They seem to offer a way of turning the pension into cash now; they do it by getting you to take your pension early. You thus release the fund and roughly a quarter of it can be taken as a tax-free lump sum. The rest has to be used to buy a pension for life.

These schemes are legal. But taking your pension early:

- reduces the pension you have in older age;
- uses up the lump sum; and
- costs money in fees to an adviser.

The Financial Services Authority is very concerned about some of the companies that sell these schemes to unlock your pension in your 50s. The FSA says that they are suitable only in exceptional cases. It produced figures in 2003 which showed the devastating effects of taking your pension early. It says a man of 53 who had a pension fund of £11,256 could wait until he was 65 and get a pension of £1,824 a year. Yet if he unlocked his pension at 53 he would get a lump sum of £4,337, and his pension would only be £340 a year at 65. So he was giving up nearly £1,500 a year – for life – in exchange for a cash amount of £4,337 at 53.

The financial advisers who arrange these schemes make their living by taking a fee, so part of your pension pot will benefit them rather than you. The FSA has warned companies in this field that they must give adequate warnings in their sales literature and it has warned that it may fine or close down firms which mis-sell these products. In February 2004 it fined one company £175,000 for misleading advertising and serious failings in the advice it gave to 5,000 customers.

So before you consider cashing in your pension early, ask what the adviser's fees are and make sure you will you have enough to live on in retirement. It is not worth giving up your long-term security in exchange for a relatively small amount of cash now. If you do want to draw your pension early, you can do it without the help of an advisor at all. Just tell your employer or insurance company and explore the options.

If you are under 50 there is no legal way to unlock your pension. That does not stop some crooks from trying to sell you schemes to do it. Do not get caught by them.

STARTING ANOTHER PENSION

Although taking your only or main pension early is not a good idea, if you have a job or a good income in your 50s, you can use the pension rules to save tax and build up an income for your old age, especially if you pay higher-rate tax. With 'immediate vesting pensions' you buy a pension, benefit from the tax relief, and then immediately draw the pension and take the tax-free lump sum.

The arithmetic works like this. You pay in at least £2,808 to a stakeholder pension – more in some circumstances. The Chancellor pays in tax relief of £792, so there is £3,600 in your pension fund. You can take a quarter of that as a tax-free lump sum, which is £900, leaving £2,700 invested in the pension at a cost to you of just £1,908. If you are a higher-rate taxpayer you can claim back a further £648 in tax relief, meaning that it has cost you just £1,260 to get £2,700 in a pension fund. At current annuity rates in your 50s that will bring in around £100 a year index-linked for life – a return of around 8 per cent index-linked. You cannot get such a guaranteed deal anywhere else. Even basic-rate taxpayers are getting 5.25 per cent.

Because this can only be done through an insurance company, there will, of course, be charges taken out of it and you will end up with something less than this 8 per cent. Nevertheless, it is a good deal if you have the income and can afford it; especially if you are a higher-rate taxpayer. You should get financial advice from a reputable financial adviser to pick the best company to do this with.

SMALL FUNDS

If a particular pension fund you have tracked down is less than £2,500, then you can cash it in. The same is true of an occupational pension that is less than £260 a year. The first 25 per cent is tax free and the rest is taxed at 35 per cent. Under new government plans, this rule will be changed in April 2006. Then you will be able to cash in a fund of less than £15,000. However, there will be two restrictions: you can only cash in a fund once you have reached 60; and you can only do it in one tax year. In that year you can cash in any number of funds as long as the total value is no more than £15,000. You can do what you like with this cash, although it is probably sensible to use at least some of it to buy yourself a pension. It will be taxed as income in the year you receive it.

There are two advantages of doing it this way rather than buying a pension annuity:

- You can keep the money in cash or a fixed return investment for as long as you like and use it in emergencies while it is there.
- If you do buy an annuity, it will be taxed more favourably. (There is more about these 'purchased life annuities' on page 24.)

PENSIONS IN PERIL

Final salary schemes used to be considered the Rolls Royce of pensions – well designed, guaranteed, and they never went wrong. If a company offered such a pension the advice was always 'join it'. Not any more. In the last few years a crisis has hit these pensions. The funds to pay them have turned out to be inadequate. Dozens of employers are closing these schemes to new entrants and some are closing them altogether. Tens of thousands of people have found the pension promises they were made have evaporated. Although the

Government has taken some action and promised more, there are fears that the changes will be too little and too late.

If you are in a public sector scheme – in other words, your employer is the State, either the national or local government or you work for the NHS or an employer funded by taxpayers – then your scheme is still safe. Your pension is guaranteed by taxpayers. But outside the public sector, these pensions are in peril.

A final salary scheme is a promise to pay a pension for life linked to the individual's salary. If you are in a final salary scheme, your employer will pay a percentage of your salary into a separate pension fund. In most cases you will pay in as well. Typically, your employer will pay in just over 9 per cent of your pay.

The fund is managed by independent trustees who will include directors of the company and, usually, staff representatives. The fund is entirely separate from the company and is invested to maximise the return on the money so that the pensions that have been promised can be paid. However, if the fund is not sufficient to pay the pensions then the company has to find the money needed. In other words, your employer has to stand behind the promises it has made to you about the pensions that will be paid. Today a growing number of companies fear that they will have to step in to prop up ailing pension funds which have suffered several damaging blows.

From the mid 1950s pension funds invested their money mainly in shares. During the last half of the 20th Century, especially the last 25 years, shares only went one way – up. The result was that pension funds seemed to have plenty of money. Actuaries confidently said that they had more money than they needed to meet their pension promises.

The funds seemed so buoyant that the Government intervened. In 1987 the Government stepped in and told pension funds that if they had more than 105 per cent of what the Inland Revenue thought they needed to meet their pension promises, then they had to reduce the fund. Companies normally did this by cutting their own contributions rather than those of their employees. Over the years from 1987 to 2001 companies withheld £19 billion. In addition, some companies kept back even more – no figures for this loss exist. Many companies used pension scheme surpluses to make people redundant and offer them enhanced pensions – no-one knows how much this cost pension funds either.

In 1995 the Government also decreed that from April 1997 any pension earned from that time must have some protection against inflation. It is called Limited Price Indexation (LPI) and the benefits earned from that year have to be increased by inflation up to a maximum of 5 per cent a year (and it can be more). This promise is very costly, but the funds seemed so buoyant after a long stock market rise that the money seemed to be there.

In 1997, Chancellor Gordon Brown in his first Budget said 'Many pension funds are in substantial surplus … so this is the right time to … abolish tax credits paid to pension funds'. Losing this tax relief cost pension funds an estimated £5 billion a year (although the restructuring of Corporation Tax a year later offset this by around £3.5bn) and, of course, came at exactly the same time as LPI kicked in. Although changes to company taxation gave some of this money back to employers, there was no mechanism to return it to the pension fund.

This triple whammy from two governments meant that pension funds lost the cushion they had built up during the good times, leaving them vulnerable to a sudden stock market fall. What happened next? From January 2000 to March 2003 the stock market tumbled to less than half its value.

Over the same period actuaries began to realise that life expectancy was increasing more rapidly than they had expected. That meant pensions had to be paid for longer and that, of course, meant that a bigger fund was needed for each pension that had been promised. So the actuaries got to work and increased their estimates of the cost of providing a pension for life. The accountants got in on the act too – a new accountancy standard (called FRS17) was introduced which meant that pension fund liabilities had to be clearly shown in company accounts. Although the full implementation of this rule was deferred, companies still had to put the figures as a note to their accounts. The size of the liabilities was frightening.

In 2002 the Confederation of British Industry estimated that the pension funds of UK companies were £160 billion short of what they needed to meet their pension promises. The rise in the stock market has cut that deficit, but it is still estimated to be well over £100 billion. Many large firms have already pumped hundreds of millions into their ailing pension schemes – Glaxo SmithKline and AstraZeneca paid nearly a billion pounds between them in 2002 to prop up their pension funds, for example. Overall, companies with final salary schemes predict that their average contribution will have to rise from 9.2 per cent of each employee's salary to 15.5 per cent. In many cases employees have paid their share of increased costs too.

It is no wonder then that many employers are trying to move away from final salary pension schemes. After all, the value of stock market investments is a gamble, but pensions are guaranteed amounts. So liabilities which are certain have to be paid from funds that are anything but. FRS17 did not make the problem worse, but it did make it much more apparent.

The result is that final salary pension schemes are being seen as a luxury that more and more companies feel they cannot afford. A former chairman of the National Association of Pension Funds, an actuary called Peter Thompson, said recently that two thirds of them were at risk. Other analysts expect them to have all but disappeared, at least from the private sector, within ten years. As they close, their members may be left with broken pension promises.

Closing down a final salary scheme

There may be three stages to closing down a final salary pension scheme. The first step is to close the fund to new members of staff. Existing staff carry on paying in and keep the promise of a pension related to their pay. But new members of staff cannot join, although they are normally offered the alternative of a different sort of company scheme – usually a money purchase scheme (see page 28) which offers them no guaranteed pension. That almost always results in both them and the employer paying in less: on average the amount going in falls by a third. One in six final salary schemes in the private sector and one in ten in the public sector are now closed to new entrants. BT, Britain's biggest pension fund, recently took that step.

The next step is to close the final salary scheme to all staff, including those already in it. That may follow a few years after stage one, when there are more staff outside the scheme than in it. Many smaller companies have already taken this step. For example, in 2002 accountants Ernst & Young closed its 1,500 member scheme. When that happens the fund continues but people in the scheme get their benefits 'frozen'. The closer you are to retirement, the less you will lose. But for everyone, the pension will be less than was promised.

The final step is to wind up the scheme – that can happen either at the choice of the company or inevitably if it goes bust. In June 2003 the Government announced that all companies, which were not insolvent and which chose to close their scheme, had to put money into the pension fund to ensure that there was sufficient to meet their pension promises. Regulations to bring this into law have recently been made. But there is a loophole. If that contribution would be so big that paying would risk pushing the company into insolvency, then it can avoid this obligation, as long as the pension fund trustees agree. The Pensions Advisory Service (OPAS) has warned that companies may use this as a loophole to refuse to stand behind their pension promises when they choose to wind up a scheme.

When a company goes out of business

In the USA pension obligations are driving some companies to the wall. The photographic company Polaroid, and one of America's oldest companies, Bethlehem Steel, both filed for insolvency protection in 2001, partly blaming the cost of employee pension and benefit promises.

So far few UK companies have gone bust because of the cost of their pension scheme. But many pension schemes have been wrecked by the company itself going bust.

When a company goes out of business, the pension trustees have a duty to act in the interests of their members. With no more money coming in, the pension promises are at risk. Under a law introduced in 1997, pensions already in payment have to be guaranteed first – although many schemes already did this. That means the fund has to be used to buy annuities to guarantee those who have already retired a pension for life. Annuity rates are low at the moment, so that is an expensive exercise. Once the lawyers, actuaries, auditors, and accountants have been paid, whatever is left in the fund is used to buy pensions for the people who have not yet retired. That is done by purchasing annuities that will start paying out when they reach pension age. Again, low annuity rates mean that these pensions are very expensive. These two factors mean that there is so little money left that people who have paid into their scheme for decades can be left with pensions worth a small fraction of what they were expecting.

It was not supposed to be like this. By law, every pension fund has to have enough money to meet what is called the Minimum Funding Requirement (MFR), but the MFR does not mean they have enough to pay the pensions their members expect. Recent experience shows a scheme which comes to an end, even if it meets the MFR, only has enough resources to buy pensions of around a third of what was promised to workers who have not yet retired.

Many schemes do not even meet the MFR. They are assessed only every three years and funds which met the MFR three years ago when share prices were higher may not meet it now. If a fund is found to be short of its MFR the company can have up to ten years to top it up (three years if it is below 90 per cent). Companies in financial difficulties seldom give priority to paying contributions into the pension fund – although new regulations may make that rarer in future. The result is that when a company goes bust the fund may be well below even the MFR and there may be nothing left to pay pensions for people who have not yet retired.

The people affected are a minority – the Government does not collect figures on how many people have lost the pension they have been promised when their company has gone bust – but the figure probably lies between 20,000 and 40,000. This has to be set against the 10 million currently paying in – or who have paid in – to a private sector final salary scheme. So the risk, at less than half of one per cent, is not great. But for those it hits it can be devastating.

Remember that public sector schemes are not affected by these problems. If you are a public sector worker in one, stay in; if not, join it.

PENSION PROTECTION

The Government is introducing a new insurance scheme called the Pension Protection Fund. Every pension scheme will have to pay an annual premium into the Fund, at first related to the number of members but later also related to how secure the fund is. When a company goes out of business, the Fund will take over the pension assets and meet the pension promises. The scheme will not start until April 2006 and the Government has said it will not be backdated. So people whose employer has already gone bust – or which goes bust before that date – will not be helped. Even when it is in place, there will be limits on what it can pay out.

There are also doubts over the viability of the Pension Protection Fund. In the USA a similar scheme has existed since 1975, but it has come under huge financial strains as a growing number of company failures has led to a rapid growth in its costs. Its deficit is now around £6.25 billion and some officials say it will be necessary for the Federal Government to step in to support the pensions promises it has taken over. In the UK the Government has refused to give an assurance that it will support the scheme if it fails.

Meanwhile, campaigners are taking the Government to court to try to force it to take action. They claim that the Government is breaking a 23-year-old European Union law (Article 8 of the 1980 Employment Insolvency Directive) which requires governments to protect employees' pension rights when companies go bust. They also say it is breaking the Human Rights Act by taking away their right to the 'property' of a pension. These cases could take years.

Stuck in the middle of all this are employees who want to know what to do. Already, the problems facing pension schemes are discouraging people from joining them. That could be an expensive mistake. It used to be the one piece of financial advice that was always right – if your company operates a final salary pension scheme, join it. Now that advice has to be tempered with a warning – if your employer goes bust, then the money you have paid in over the years may be lost. But it is still good advice for the vast majority of people.

Anyone in their 50s who works for a company that offers a final salary pension scheme should join it, whatever their age, and people approaching retirement should never leave such a scheme. But everyone must be aware that if the company goes bust – certainly before the Pension Protection Fund begins in April 2006 – and they have not retired, their pension could be at risk.

If you are in a final salary pension scheme it is worth lobbying your trustees – at least one of whom must be an employee like you – to see what their plans are. Companies can always pull the plug if they feel they cannot afford the contributions, although new rules may make that less common than in the recent past.

Remember that there are other ways to save up for retirement – either through a stakeholder pension or AVCs (see pages 29–30), which will normally be separate from the company scheme and safe if it goes bust, or through ISAs or other savings plans. But beware any advisor who suggests that you move your money from a company scheme to a personal pension – the chances are that they will make money from that move and you will lose.

Of course, the worry of insolvency does not exist for public sector workers, so they should always join. Nor do these problems affect money purchase or defined contribution schemes. If your company has one of those and puts in money on your behalf it would be foolish not to join.

ALTERNATIVES TO A PENSION

The poor performance of the stock market and the effect that has had on the size of pensions – not to mention the collapse of some pension schemes – has led a lot of people to question the wisdom of relying on traditional pensions for our financial needs in later life. There are other ways of saving up.

Pensions, nevertheless, have two advantages:

The money going in is free of tax All other forms of saving comes out of your taxed income. For example, if you want to put £250 into a saving plan, that money you have earned has already had tax deducted. So to have £250 you must have earned £320 if you are a basic-rate taxpayer, or £417 if you are a higher-rate taxpayer, to have £250 to put into a savings account.

If you put £250 into a pension plan, however, it is out of your income before tax is deducted. So you can put £320 in if you are a basic-rate taxpayer and it will only cost you £250 out of your available money. If you are a higher-rate taxpayer you can put in £417 and only be £250 poorer. So all that extra money is earning interest and most of the growth is tax free too. Employers also put in contributions, in almost all final salary schemes and most money purchase ones, and they are tax free for them as well. These huge subsidies to pension contributions costs the country nearly £14 billion a year.

Because the money going in is tax free, when you draw your pension the whole of the income is taxable. At that time of life you may well be paying a lower rate of tax. Some people may get tax relief at 22 per cent and only pay tax at 10 per cent or even pay no tax at all in retirement. Others may get tax relief at 40 per cent when they pay into a pension but are only taxed at 22 per cent when they draw the pension. The only times it may work to your disadvantage is if you pay a lower rate of tax paying in and a higher rate in retirement, but even then there is a tax-free lump sum you can take. So normally the tax relief works to your advantage or is neutral (ie you pay tax at the same rate in work and retirement).

The money in a pension is locked up until you reach at least 50 and later in some cases. That is a big advantage for most people, who might be tempted to use it during those expensive times of adult life – you need a deposit for a house, your children go to university, you have a big debt to clear, you lose your job. The pension rules keep your fund safe until you retire and also specify strictly what it can be used for. The Government sees that as the price we pay for the advantages of tax relief.

Of course, some people see these strict rules as a problem. There are moments in life when the money locked up in your pension scheme would be very useful. The rule which says you have to use at least three quarters of your fund to buy an annuity – certainly by the age of 75 – is indeed very restrictive. But for most people most of the time the tough protection helps them avoid temptation.

ISAs

Some people have seen Individual Savings Accounts (ISAs) as an alternative to saving in a pension. Money going into an ISA is paid out of your taxed income; but when you cash the ISA in or spend some of the growth it has earned, that is completely free of tax. So an ISA is the mirror image of a pension – taxed going in and tax free coming out. There are two disadvantages compared with a pension. Because the money going in is taxed, less goes in for the same cost to you and there is less in your investment earning money. Second, the tax timing is the wrong way round for using as a pension. If you take the money out in retirement, you are likely to be paying tax at a lower rate than when you pay it in. It is the opposite for a pension.

There is now another big disadvantage. If you invest the money in shares, then the tax-free growth is restricted. Since April 2004 dividends are in effect taxed at the basic rate and the only advantage is for higher-rate taxpayers or the small number of people who pay Capital Gains Tax. This tax does not apply to ISA investments which are not in shares: you can get ISAs which are invested in bonds or other products where the growth is all tax-free. Of course, they are also much more flexible than a pension – you can use the money tax free at any age and for any purpose. There is a limit to how much goes in – currently £7,000 a year – but that is far more than most people invest in their pension. (There is more information about ISAs on pages 22–23.)

PROPERTY

As share prices have stalled, so the price of domestic property has soared. Rising property prices have meant that a growing number of people who are unable or unwilling to buy have been keen to rent a home. Step forward 'Buy to Let'. In the past it was difficult to borrow money to buy a property to rent out rather than to live in it yourself. But then the Association of Residential Letting Agents (ARLA) got together with some mortgage lenders to work out a way that everyone could make money from rising property prices and the strong rental market. Buy to Let is now well established and it works quite simply. You identify a property that you want to buy in order to let it out. You find a deposit of at least 15 per cent of the price of the property (up to 25 per cent with some lenders). You borrow the rest and become the landlord and let it out.

How Buy to Let works

Buying to let does not suit everyone. It is more like trading than investing: you have to buy the capital asset and pay the expenses of running it and collecting the income. However, professionals in the field estimate that you can make a return of up to 10 per cent a year; more in some areas and on some types of property. Of course, you can make less or even lose money. Borrowing to get a good return is always a dangerous business. The debt will have to be paid regardless of the performance of the asset. So it is important that you take care of all the details first. It is a long-term investment – ten years is a sensible timescale.

Normal residential mortgages do not let you rent out the property, but many major lenders now offer mortgages specifically for buying to let. Normally you will take out an interest-only mortgage and repay the capital when you sell the property in the future. The big difference with Buy to Let mortgages is that you have to find a big deposit. Typically, you can only borrow up to 75 per cent of the purchase price, although some will go as high as 85 per cent. That means you have to find the balance yourself from savings or other resources. You will also have to pay a percentage commission to the agent that arranges it – many Buy to Let deals are only available through brokers. That fee can be high and is generally higher than the fees charged to people taking out a mortgage for the home they live in; but set against that, a broker may be able to find you a better deal than you could get yourself.

Interest rates are higher; usually around 1 per cent to 1.5 per cent higher than the best you can get for buying a home you will live in. Fixed rate mortgages are attractive for Buy to Let because your costs are fixed and that gives more certainty about the arithmetic when you compare your rent with your outgoings. With a fixed rate, look carefully at what rate you will be charged when the fix runs out, and avoid any mortgage that penalises you for switching to another provider after the fixed rate comes to an end.

In November 2003 the Bank of England began to put up rates after cutting them in July that year to 3.5 per cent – their lowest level since 1955. They went up again in February and May 2004 and most economists are predicting further rises perhaps to around 5 per cent in 2004–2005. So build in a rate rise, perhaps to 6 per cent, to any calculations you do.

The lender will normally specify that the property can be rented out for a monthly income of around 125 or 130 per cent of the mortgage payments. When they do that calculation they may ignore any temporary discount on the interest rate. So a £100,000 property will have to bring in a rent of around £650 a month.

You should also make sure that the mortgage is flexible – in other words, that you can pay more or less each month if you want. With Buy to Let it is a good idea to make sure that you can miss a payment occasionally when the property is empty and no rent is coming in. But always try to pay more in subsequent months – or in advance – to make up the difference.

Apart from the deposit, you will also need money to furnish the property. Even 'unfurnished' lettings may need decorating and you will have to provide carpets, curtains, light bulbs and a fully equipped kitchen and bathroom. Any fitted gas appliances, such as fires and boilers, will have to comply with stringent safety regulations. Electrical fittings and appliances will have to be properly installed by qualified contractors and safe. Smoke and carbon monoxide detectors are a good idea. If you decide to furnish the property, the law demands that all soft furnishings comply with modern safety standards.

In the past, properties that were let 'unfurnished' gave tenants more rights. That is no longer true. Lettings are now for a period of six months and can be terminated by either side at that date, so there should be no fears about getting rid of tenants as long as you get a proper tenancy agreement.

You should also set something aside for the inevitable repairs, renewals and decorations. A good-looking home will be let more quickly, and it is very important to keep the home occupied; too many empty months – 'voids' is the jargon – and you will find the year's profit disappearing very rapidly.

As with any product you are trying to sell, it is vital to do your research. Many people consider buying to let in an area where they would like to live – possibly retire to or keep as a second home. But that is not a good idea. An area where you may want to retire is not necessarily a good area for Buy to Let. The property should be looked on purely as a business deal, an investment, and that means choosing a place where your money will produce a good return. If your own area or somewhere nearby is good for letting, then that may be a good place to start. Remember that you may have to visit the property a lot (to see tenants, deal with emergencies or meet your local agent, if you have one); but whether the property is in a good area for letting is a more important factor than your convenience – a lot of Greater London and many other major cities are good. Convenient areas for motorway travel or commuting, places where companies have their headquarters, university towns or places close to major hospitals, all have good potential for letting. A quick trip round local letting agents will tell you if there is a market in that area. These are not necessarily the same as estate agents. Many of them belong to the Association of Residential Letting Agents (ARLA), which ensures its members are competent to manage rented property. They can give you advice about the local market, including what kind of property is in demand and what kind is not. Most do not charge for basic advice.

One thing you should avoid is buying to let in a block of flats or a residential development which has been sold for that purpose. You will be competing against other landlords trying to let identical property to much the same tenants. That can only bring down prices. The value of these properties is often exaggerated anyway. It is very important that you do your own research from the rental adverts in local newspapers, as well as talking to several agents and thinking carefully about the essential rule of supply and demand – who will want to rent the property from you, and what is the supply of similar places in that area?

Once you have chosen your property and bought it, you will need to make sure it is fit to let. You can get help with this and other aspects of letting from a local residential letting agent. Many people who look on Buy to Let as an investment do not want to become a landlord in the real sense of the word. So they are happy to treat the cost of an agent as an overhead. An agent will find tenants, take up references and organise all the details of the letting, including the tenancy agreement, taking an inventory and making sure that gas, electricity and water companies know who the new occupier is and when they began their tenancy. The agent will also hold the deposit and check the property at the end of the tenancy before handing it back. To do all this, they will charge around 10 per cent of the rent during the period of the let. If you want them to manage the property fully, which means that they will act in your place and deal with problems and repairs, then they will charge another 5 per cent or so of the rent. Some charge more; others may charge less.

Many people who go into Buy to Let are cautious investors. They want to know where their money is, and there is nothing like walking by a property and feeling that sense of ownership! Apart from the profit you make from the rent, you can probably look forward to owning an appreciating asset. As the value of shares fell by around 50 per cent between the start of 2000 and Spring 2003, house prices rose by around 55 per cent. Put another way – if you had invested £100,000 in January 2000 in the stock market and another £100,000 in UK property, then by March 2003 the shares would have would have been worth around £48,000 but the property would have been worth around £155,000.

In 2003, the price of houses and flats rose again and the prospects for the future are further rises. Although every year commentators and economists say 'it cannot go on at that rate forever', so far prices have continued to rise above predictions every year. One reason is that there is a shortage of homes and a growing demand. The most basic rule of economics predicts rising prices in those circumstances. Of course, no investment is completely free of risk, but buying to let can be a lot more enjoyable than poring over share prices. Owning property as a way to wealth is the origin of the 18th Century phrase 'safe as houses'.

Be very aware, however, that in any new area of investment – especially one that is not regulated – there will be crooks around who want your money. Be very cautious about any sort of scheme that offers high or risk-free returns in property. Such things do not exist. Buying to let is risky and nothing is guaranteed. It takes a lot of research in advance and continual work – and some luck – afterwards for it to pay off.

More information is available from the Association of Residential Letting Agents on 0845 345 5752 or at www.arla.co.uk/btl You can compare Buy to Let mortgages at www.moneyfacts.co.uk

MANAGING
YOUR MONEY

This part of the book is mainly about cutting your expenditure. In your 50s you may have got into habits you are not even aware of, but which could be costing you money. Perhaps you pay out regular expenses that you have got used to and never check, or you have some debts and never worry about exactly what they cost you, or you pay tax and never even wonder if it is right. This section can help you sort that out. It also looks at financial advice – how to find someone you trust – and concludes with a reminder about making a will.

In this section:

CUTTING TAX

- Income Tax
- Tax on savings
- National Insurance
- Capital Gains Tax
- Inheritance Tax

DEBT

- Mortgages
- Credit cards
- Bank loans
- APR
- Bad debt

INSURANCE

- Life insurance
- Illness and disability
- Bad insurance
- Good insurance

FINANCIAL ADVICE

- Independent Financial Advisers
- Agents
- New procedures
- Commission
- Choosing an IFA
- Protect yourself
- Complaining
- Compensation

MAKING A WILL

CUTTING TAX

People in their 50s pay the same tax as anyone else – there are no special concessions. However, it is also a time of great change, and when your circumstances change your tax can be calculated wrongly. So it is always worth checking your tax. There are also ways to cut tax that you may not know about.

INCOME TAX

In the tax year 2004–2005 everyone can have £4,745 a year of income before any tax is due. Extra tax relief for married couples was abolished in April 2000 except where one member of the couple was born before 6 April 1935. So you will be eligible only if you are married to someone who is aged 69 or more.

If you are an employee, then your tax is deducted from your pay through the tax code. The code is a way of collecting tax, not assessing it, and it can be wrong. So it is always worth checking your tax code. For people under 65 it is normally 474L – which simply means that your tax allowance is the standard £4,745 lower rate. But if you stop or start work during the year, especially if you have a period without work, your tax code may be wrong. So if your income changes during the year it is well worth checking your tax at the end of the year.

If your code is anything but 474L in 2004–2005 then it is worth checking. Some codes should give particular concern:

- **BR** means that tax is deducted at the basic rate – ask why.
- **0T** means that your income is taxed with no tax allowance – ask why.

- **K** before the number means that you have a 'negative' code; in other words, your earnings are being taxed at a higher rate than normal. This should only happen if you have more than £4,745 untaxed income, so your earnings are taxed at a higher rate to include some of the tax due on your untaxed income as well.

Always get such codes checked. Apart from a K code, the higher your code number the less tax you are paying.

If you are an employee there are not many expenses you can claim against your tax. But there are some – and they are relatively unknown.

Uniforms and tools

Some jobs allow you to claim a fixed annual allowance for the upkeep of tools you need for your job or a uniform which you have to wear and keep clean yourself. These allowances are small, ranging from £30 for bench hands in the printing industry to £165 for carpenters on passenger liners. Allowances for care of uniforms are typically around £40 – for bank employees for example. Remember that this is a tax allowance, so it means that, for example, £40 of your income is not taxed, which is worth just £8.80 a year for a basic-rate taxpayer.

This allowance is called concession A1. The full list of allowances is set out in booklet IR1 *Extra Statutory Concessions*. Copies are available from tax offices or you can also download it from www.inlandrevenue.gov.uk/leaflets/c13.htm

Professional subscriptions

If you belong to a professional organisation as part of your job, or subscribe to a journal that you need for your work, you may be able to claim tax relief on the cost. There are thousands of organisations and journals on the list. The range is enormous – from the British Association of Art Therapists to the Institute of Wood Science. They tend to be biased towards the professions; the British Medical Association is included, for example, but all traditional trade unions are excluded. But if your job requires you to subscribe to an organisation or a journal, then it is worth checking if you can claim tax relief on the whole subscription. As these can be a couple of hundred pounds a year, the tax saving can be well worthwhile.

The concession is officially called Deduction for Fees and Subscriptions Paid to Professional Bodies or Learned Societies. For some reason the list of those that are approved is called List 3. You can buy it but it is much easier to check the more up-to-date list online at www.inlandrevenue.gov.uk/list3

Car travel

Journeys to and from the place where you work cannot be set against tax. If your employer pays the cost, then you have to pay Income Tax and National Insurance on that money. The one exception is if your employer pays for a taxi home if you have to work after 9pm – but the concession only applies if such late work is occasional and unpredictable.

Journeys you make in the course of your work can be paid for by your employer and no tax is due on the money. Also, if you drive your own car you can be paid up to 40p a mile without it counting as part of your pay. So no tax or National Insurance is due on it. If your employer is mean and does not pay you anything – or pays you less than 40p a mile – then you can claim the difference as a tax-free allowance. So if you drive 1,000 miles and your employer pays you 25p a mile, not only is the £250 free of tax and National Insurance but you can also claim another £150 of income as a tax-free allowance.

Every employer deals with one tax office. Ask your payment department which one it is. Contact that office about claiming a repayment of any overpaid tax.

TAX ON SAVINGS

Millions of people pay tax on their savings which they could avoid. The last time the Government gave any figures, it said that four million people were owed £300 million in overpaid tax on their savings. The reason is simple. Basic-rate tax of 20 per cent is automatically deducted from any interest earned on money in a bank or building society account. That means if you earn £100 in interest, £20 is deducted automatically and sent to the Treasury. For many people, this is a convenient way to pay the tax due. But for millions it is a rip-off. They either pay no tax at all and should have nothing deducted, or they pay tax at the lower rate of 10 per cent and should only have half the tax deducted.

If you or your partner lose your job or suffer a big fall in income, something that can often happen in your 50s, then it is worth checking that too much tax is not being deducted from your savings.

If you are due to pay no tax at all, then you can register to have your interest paid gross. You do this on form R85. That should ensure that tax is not deducted in future. It is likely that you will also have been wrongly paying tax on your interest in the past. You can claim that back for six years – back to 1998–1999 – using another form (R40).

You also have to use R40 if your income is low enough so that you only have to pay tax at 10 per cent. Anyone with an income between £4,745 and £6,765 is having tax deducted from their savings interest at twice the correct rate. You can claim it back using R40 for past years. You normally have to wait to the end of the tax year to claim this tax back; but if it is more than £50 you can claim it at any time.

You can get these forms from your local Inland Revenue Enquiry Centre or download them from the IR website at www.inlandrevenue.gov.uk You can get more information about claiming tax back from the IR website too, or call the TaxBack Helpline on 0845 980 0645. A useful leaflet called IR110 *Bank and Building Society Interest: A Guide for Savers* is available from tax offices, the IR Orderline on 08459 000 404 or the website.

If you have a spouse or partner and one of you pays no tax or only pays tax at the lower rate, you could consider moving savings into the name of that person. In that way you avoid paying tax on the interest earned by your savings. Remember, however, that the savings then become that person's property. If this would cause any difficulties, don't do it.

A couple with a joint bank or building society account can still save tax if one of them is a non-taxpayer. If you let the bank know, it should credit half the interest gross and the other half with tax deducted. If it will not do that, then the non-taxpayer can reclaim the overpaid tax at the end of the tax year on form R40.

The other way to save tax on your savings is to put some of your cash into an ISA. The interest is paid tax free to everyone. (There is more information about ISAs on page 8.)

NATIONAL INSURANCE

If you earn at least £91 a week in 2004–2005 (£395 per month), then National Insurance contributions will be deducted from your pay by your employer. If you earn less than £91 a week, you do not have to pay contributions. But if you earn at least £79 (£343 per month), you will get a contribution credited to you for that week. If you earn less than £79 a week, no credits will be paid and you will have a gap in your record. (See pages 151–154 for more information about paying extra contributions.)

Contributions are normally 11 per cent of earnings between £91 and £610 a week (less if you are in an occupational pension scheme which is contracted out of the State Second Pension) and 1 per cent of earnings above £610 a week.

If you are earning just below the Lower Earnings Limit (£79), it could be worth increasing your hours to bring you above it, so that you start building up National Insurance entitlement without actually paying anything. Your employer may resist this, however, as it does have to pay National Insurance contributions.

Some married women pay a lower rate of 4.85 per cent on earnings between £91 and £610. These contributions are a complete waste of money. They earn you nothing – you get no right to Jobseeker's Allowance if you are unemployed and no right to a State Pension. But they can cost you £25 a week or more. In most cases you would be better off switching to the full rate of Class 1 contributions. Although you will pay more, the contributions will count towards Jobseeker's Allowance, towards Sickness Benefit, and towards earning you a bigger State Pension – including State Second Pension (S2P) if you are not already paying into a company or stakeholder pension. You can opt back into paying full contributions using the form at the back of Inland Revenue leaflet CA13 *National Insurance Contributions for Married Women with Reduced Elections*.

Contributions have to be paid until the week before you reach State Pension age – normally 65 but many women currently in their 50s will reach pension age between 60 and 64 (see page 151). Many people complain about paying National Insurance contributions in their late 50s and 60s because they feel they have paid enough to get a full State Pension and that paying any more is a waste of money. However, the rules do not allow people who have paid 'enough' contributions to stop paying them. They are due right up to State Pension age regardless of how complete or otherwise your National Insurance record is.

Self-employed people have to pay what are called Class 2 contributions of £2.05 a week (in 2004–2005) if their income is at least £4,215 in the year. Below that they can apply for what is called 'small earnings exception' but it has to be applied for. Get Inland Revenue leaflet CA02 *National Insurance Contributions for Self-employed People with Small Earnings* and fill in the form at the back. You can download it from the Inland Revenue website (www.inlandrevenue.gov.uk).

Self-employed people also have to pay Class 4 contributions of 8 per cent on their annual profits between £4,745 and £31,720 and 1 per cent on all profits above £31,720.

Class 2 contributions have to be paid until the week before you reach State Pension age. Class 4 contributions have to be paid for the whole tax year in which you reach pension age.

If you do more than one job, it is possible that you will pay too much National Insurance. The rule is that you cannot pay more altogether than if you earned the same amount and worked for just one employer. You can claim back overpaid National Insurance contributions from your tax office. Your employer will tell you which office this is. If you do several jobs, each paying below the Lower Earnings Limit (£79 in 2004–2005), you don't pay National Insurance contributions on any of them, but you also don't build up any National Insurance entitlement.

CAPITAL GAINS TAX

Very few people pay Capital Gains Tax (CGT) – and most of them are pretty well off. In 2002–2003, fewer than 100,000 paid it, compared with nearly 30 million who paid Income Tax. But because it is so unexpected, CGT can suddenly appear from nowhere.

The principle is simple enough. If you buy something at one price and sell it for a profit, the gain in value can be taxed. It was originally introduced to make sure people could not avoid Income Tax by making gains rather than being paid income. Needless to say, the tax is now very complex and hedged around with exceptions and strange rules. Each year you are allowed to make a certain amount of gains before any tax is due. In 2004–2005 that amount is £8,200 and a husband and wife can make that much each.

Exemptions

The home you live in is normally completely exempt from CGT when you sell it or give it away. To be exempt the house must have been your main residence throughout the time you owned it. If it has more than half a hectare of ground (ie about an acre), then CGT may be due on the rise in value on the part of the land that exceeds that amount.

If you own and live in two properties, you can nominate one of them to be your 'main' residence. You need to do this within two years of acquiring the second property. If the other property has been occupied by a dependent relative rent-free since before 6 April 1988, it may be exempt from CGT.

If you have a lodger in the home you own, who shares a kitchen and bathroom and living space with you and who lives as a member of the family, you should not have to pay CGT when you sell the property. However, if you let part of your home to someone who does not live as a member of your family, CGT may be payable. That applies even if the rent is exempt from Income Tax under the Rent a Room scheme (see pages 184–185). The gain on which CGT will be calculated uses a fairly complex formula related to the proportion of the property that is rented and the period of letting relative to the total period of ownership. There is also a special exemption called 'Private Residence Relief' which may mean that no CGT is payable. Inland Revenue leaflet IR87 *Letting and Your Home* explains how this relief works.

If you use part of your home exclusively for business purposes, then a proportion of the property may also be liable to CGT when you sell it.

Other things are completely free of CGT. They include:

- private cars (even historic and valuable ones);
- government investments, such as National Savings and gilts; and
- personal belongings worth up to £6,000 each.

Paying CGT

If you do make a gain in the year of more than £8,200, then the excess is added to your income and taxed as if it was income.

If the asset was bought on 6 April 1998 or later, then the gain you have made is reduced or 'tapered' depending on how long you have owned the asset. For example, for non-business assets owned for five years since April 1998, 85 per cent of the gain will be chargeable, and if they are held for 10 or more years the figure will be 60 per cent. If you acquired the asset before April 1998, then a different system called 'indexation' applies to the gain over the period from when you acquired the asset to 5 April 1998. If you got it before

31 March 1982 indexation only applies from that date. The taper will apply to gains after 5 April 1998. There is a more rapid taper for business assets.

Certain expenses can also be deducted, including the cost of acquiring or disposing of the asset, or of improving it (by adding an extension to a let property for example). Your total capital gains in a year can be reduced if you have also made capital losses – for example if you bought shares which are now worth less and you sell them. Losses from earlier years can be carried forward to future years. If your overall net gain is £8,200 or less, there will be no CGT to pay. If you do make a CGT loss, remember to tell the Inland Revenue – otherwise you may not be able to carry it forward.

Assets acquired before 31 March 1982 involve slightly different calculations. If you have them and make a capital gain you should get advice from an accountant or tax adviser.

Recently some mutual insurance companies have been sold and members of the company have received large windfalls from the proceeds. If windfalls – added to any other capital gains – exceed £8,200 in the tax year, then CGT will be due. The Inland Revenue argument is that it cost you nothing to become a member of the mutual company, but that membership is now worth a lot of money. So whatever the current value of the membership it has grown from nothing and that is a capital gain. These gains can be reduced if the company borrows the money back off you and pays you interest on it, allowing you to cash in the loan each year in chunks that are below the CGT limit.

There is no CGT on transfers between husband and wife. So if you are married, you can double the amount you cash in each year. Gift £8,200 of the loan to your spouse – no CGT is payable on that, and they can then cash them in.

The rise in value of shares, unit trust units and shares in Open Ended Investment Companies (OEICs) counts as a capital gain when they are sold. You cannot avoid this tax by simply giving them away. If you give shares to someone – apart from your spouse – then the difference between the price you paid and their current market value is treated as a capital gain. If it exceeds your allowances, then you will be liable for CGT. So there are dangers in giving away shares or assets that may have grown in value as a way of reducing future Inheritance Tax liability.

For more information, see Inland Revenue leaflet CGT1 *Capital Gains Tax: An Introduction* or contact your tax office. You can also find out more on the Inland Revenue website (www.inlandrevenue.gov.uk).

INHERITANCE TAX

People in their 50s naturally start worrying about the Inheritance Tax their heirs may have to pay when they die. Many 50-somethings also have to get to grips with it when a parent or other relative dies. It is worth remembering, however, that the vast majority of estates are free of this tax. In 2002–2003 less than 1 death in 20 led to an Inheritance Tax payment – just 25,000 estates out of a total of more than 530,000 deaths. There are two reasons why most estates do not have to pay Inheritance Tax:

- When the first spouse in a marriage dies, no Inheritance Tax is payable on money or property left to the surviving spouse.
- The tax does not begin until you leave at least £263,000 (in 2004–2005). Despite the rise in house prices, most people leave far less than that.

Some people do not have to pay Inheritance Tax at all. If the person's death was due to active service in the armed forces – or was hastened by it – then the whole estate is completely exempt from Inheritance Tax. This rule was used by the heirs of the fourth Duke of Westminster (the grandfather of the present Duke). They argued that his death had been hastened by cancer which was partly caused by his treatment as a prisoner in the Second World War, more than 20 years before his death. As a result, no Inheritance Tax was paid on the estate of one of the richest men in Britain.

If the total you own in cash, investments, property and belongings, and, in some cases, life insurance, is less than £263,000 then you need not worry about Inheritance Tax. If you leave more than that, then your heirs will have to pay 40 per cent of the value above £263,000. For example, on an estate worth £363,000 your heirs will have to pay 40 per cent of £100,000 or £40,000 tax. The table shows how the percentage of an estate taken by IHT grows fast as the estate value increases.

Estate	Tax	Per cent of total
£263,000	£0	0.0 per cent
£300,000	£14,800	4.9 per cent
£400,000	£54,800	13.7 per cent
£500,000	£94,800	19.0 per cent
£750,000	£194,800	26.0 per cent
£1,000,000	£294,800	29.5 per cent

To find out whether your heirs are likely to face a bill on your estate, do the following calculations:

■ Add up the value of everything you own, including your house, any investments, savings, personal property, and the value of any life insurance policies which form part of your estate (it is better to write life policies 'in trust' to avoid IHT: see page 82).

- Add to that any gifts you have made in the past seven years. You can give away up to £3,000 a year without it counting, however (see page 81).
- Take away any money owed on your mortgage, or any other debts such as unpaid bills or tax. You can also deduct the reasonable costs of your funeral.
- Take away from the total anything you intend to leave to your spouse or to charity.
- If the final amount is less than the threshold for IHT, currently £263,000, no tax will be due. If your total is more than this, it is likely that there will be IHT to pay. It is due at one rate of 40 per cent on the excess over the threshold.

Many married couples think that they need take no action on Inheritance Tax because no tax is due when the first partner dies. Yet although when the first spouse dies no tax is due on whatever their husband or wife inherits, when the second spouse dies tax is due on the whole estate. So the concession defers the tax but does not avoid it.

Reducing the bill

In fact, married couples can do more about reducing the eventual Inheritance Tax bill than single people can. That is because IHT is assessed individually. So a married couple get twice the allowances – if they are careful and separate their property while they are still alive. It is better for the first spouse to leave property to other people, using up their own tax-free limit of £263,000. Married couples can save their children tens of thousands of pounds in Inheritance Tax if they take a couple of simple steps now. It will not cost them anything and the risks are small. All they have to do is split their property and in effect double the amount they can leave without paying tax to well over half a million pounds.

Gill and Peter own a house worth around £240,000 and have investments and some cash worth another £240,000. Peter dies after a long illness and leaves everything to Gill. As his wife, she pays no Inheritance Tax. But just a year later Gill dies too, leaving the £480,000 estate to her two children, Tim and Jane. The first £263,000 is exempt from tax but the rest is taxed at 40 per cent, leaving her children with a tax bill of £86,800.

If Peter had made a will leaving the house to Gill but the rest of the property to the children, then no tax would be due when he died – the property left to his wife is free of IHT and the value of what he leaves to the children is within the £263,000 tax-free band. When Gill died she would leave the house to the children, which is also below the £263,000 limit and free of tax. So their children would inherit everything in two stages without paying any Inheritance Tax – saving £86,800.

There are drawbacks with this plan. First, the investments left to the children will no longer benefit their mother, because the gifts must be absolute. Tim and Jane are happy to pass the income on to Gill. But as they both pay tax, Jane at the higher rate, the income from the investments is reduced. Tim is also concerned that if he loses his job he will not be able to claim any means-tested benefits from the State while he has £120,000 in the bank. Not all children may be so amenable.

The plan can also work even if most of the assets are in the family home. The first thing to do is to divide the ownership of the house. Many couples own their home as what are called 'joint tenants' ('joint owners with survivorship' in Scotland). When one dies, the other simply becomes the owner of the property without formality. There is a different way of owning a home, however, which is called 'tenants in common' ('joint owners' in Scotland). Under this form of ownership, each partner owns a stated share of the property (usually half). It is simple to change to this form of ownership. Each spouse writes a letter to the other saying that in future the property will be owned as tenants in common in equal shares (in Scotland see a lawyer).

Each then makes a will leaving their share to their children. When the first partner dies, the children inherit that share of the home. They then agree to allow the surviving parent to carry on living there – that must not be a condition of the will. When the second parent dies, the children inherit the rest.

Stanley and Ethel own a home worth £440,000 as tenants in common and very little else. Stanley dies, leaving his half of the house equally between their three children James, Matthew, and Elizabeth. Ethel carries on living there until she dies and the children inherit the rest. No tax is due on either death and the children save £70,800 Inheritance Tax.

Again, there are dangers. All the children are joint owners of the home and any of them could insist it be sold at any time. If any of them divorces or goes bankrupt, then the courts could order the house to be sold to realise their share. Owning a share of the home could also prevent them from claiming Income Support, Housing Benefit or Council Tax Benefit (but not tax credits).

It is vital to make a will to ensure that your wishes are carried out. However, if you do not put proper Inheritance Tax avoidance plans in your will, then your family can effectively rewrite it after death – provided that they do so within two years of the death and provided that all the beneficiaries in the will agree. It is called a 'Deed of Variation' and is best done by a lawyer. But they will not be able to change the way the family home was owned; that has to be done by the owners while they are both alive.

Unmarried partners can also use these techniques (and they will always be tenants in common). However, there is no IHT exemption for gifts between unmarried partners and that can lead to difficulties if the first to die leaves more than the IHT limit. Leaving the surplus to their partner will not prevent tax being charged. This rule may change for some same-sex partners in late 2005 or early 2006 (see page 222).

Gifts in life

The easiest way to avoid Inheritance Tax is to give everything away and live for seven years. Any gifts made at least seven years before you die are completely exempt from Inheritance Tax. However, you have to be careful using this rule. If you give something away and still retain the use of it, then it is counted for Inheritance Tax as if you still owned it. For example, if you give your home away to your children but you continue to live in it and they don't, then the value of the home will still count as part of your estate. The Inland Revenue calls it a gift 'with reservation of benefit'. You can get round this rule by paying your children the market rent to live there. But you may not have the income to do that and they will have to pay tax on their profit and possibly Capital Gains Tax when they eventually sell the home.

You are also allowed to give away up to £3,000 each tax year without it counting as part of your estate even if you do die within seven years. A husband and wife – or unmarried parents – can each give £3,000 a year, and if you gave nothing away in the previous tax year then you can double that. So a couple who gave away nothing last year, can give away £12,000 this year without it counting as part of their estate. Even if one partner owns most of the assets, they can give £6,000 to their spouse free of any tax risk and they can each give £6,000 to their heirs. Remember, however, that you should not give your children or other heirs money that you will need yourself.

If you give shares or property which have grown in value while you owned them, then Capital Gains Tax may be payable on the gain as if you had sold it at market value (see page 76). It is safer to give away cash.

You can also give away any number of small gifts, up to £250 each, to any number of separate people. You can give up to £5,000 to a child of yours as a wedding gift – and up to £2,500 to a grandchild (or great-grandchild) or £1,000 to anyone on their marriage. If you have a high income and you give away part of that, without reducing your own lifestyle, then that is also exempt. All these allowances are personal – a husband and wife can each give these amounts.

If you have a life insurance policy that pays out on your death, make sure that the policy is what is called 'written in trust'. That means that the proceeds do not go directly to your dependants. Instead they are paid into a trust which then passes them onto your dependants; that avoids the proceeds counting as part of your estate. Ask your insurance company if your policy has been written in trust; if it has not, ask how you can change it.

Anything left in your will to a registered charity, to a university or a national museum or art gallery, or to one of the nine political parties which have at least two MPs in the UK Parliament is completely exempt from Inheritance Tax. However, giving money to charity is not a good way to avoid the tax. Your heirs will be better off having 60 per cent of something than 100 per cent of nothing.

Some insurance companies and financial consultants sell plans to reduce or avoid Inheritance Tax. Such schemes can be complicated – involving juggling the ownership of money or making gifts into or from trusts, and often involve taking out an insurance policy. These schemes are often designed to generate commission for the salesperson rather than benefit you. Before committing yourself to any scheme, be sure it has the approval of the Inland Revenue, and discuss it with an impartial professional adviser such as a solicitor or accountant. Generally they are best avoided. Setting up a trust can be a way to avoid IHT but they are expensive to set up and run and are really only suitable for people with estates worth considerably more than the quarter of a million pounds or so at which IHT starts. If you are in that position get professional advice, but be aware that the Inland Revenue has a habit of changing the rules if too many people take advantage of some new wheeze dreamed up by accountants.

For more information see Inland Revenue leaflet IHT3 *Inheritance Tax: An Introduction*. Copies are available from tax offices or from the IR Capital Taxes Orderline on 0845 234 1000.

Probate

Many people agree to be an executor of a will but find the details of what they have to do when the person dies rather a shock. Once a person has died the executors of their will are responsible for valuing all their assets, and for delivering an account of the value of the estate to the Probate Registry. At the same time they have to pay any Inheritance Tax which is due. Only then will what is called 'probate' be granted and the estate released to be sold or dispersed among the heirs. The procedure is the same in Scotland but it is called an 'inventory' and has to go to the Sheriff Clerk who grants 'confirmation'. Similar rules also apply in both jurisdictions if someone dies without a will; then the next of kin is usually appointed as an administrator to the estate.

The problem is the tax has to be paid before probate (or confirmation) is granted. Some assets of the deceased can be used to pay the tax, including National Savings & Investments products and money in an account at most banks and building societies. But if these assets are not enough – and often they will not be if a house is involved – then the executors have to borrow the money. Some High Street banks will make a loan to the executors to pay the Inheritance Tax. Make sure that you claim against the estate any interest due on this loan.

Age Concern England Factsheet 14 *Dealing with Someone's Estate* is available from the Information Line on Freephone 0800 00 99 66. You can contact the Probate and IHT Helpline on 0845 30 20 900.

DEBT

At some point we all get into debt. It is important to distinguish between different sorts of debt: it is not all bad. In particular, the debt we take on to buy a home – a mortgage – is different from any other sort of debt. So although it is better to have no debt at all, a mortgage is probably the least undesirable. The main reason is that a mortgage debt is secured; in other words, although we have the debt we also have an asset worth at least as much and which normally goes up in value. In extreme circumstances, we can use it to pay the debt off.

Good debt is debt you control. Bad debt controls you. Most people in their 50s are not as used to debt as younger people, but debt can creep up on you if your income declines or your expenses rise suddenly. Taking on debt can seem easier in the short term than reducing your standard of living or your expectations – but it is not a good idea.

Short-term debts that simply bring spending forward a few months – say up to a year – can also be good debt. We borrow some money, we buy something now, and we pay for it over a fairly short period. A golden rule of debt is that you should never pay for something over a much longer period than it is used for. So if you take two holidays a year, then you should not borrow the money to pay for them over more than six months; you should not take on debt at Christmas that is still around on 25 December next year; nor should you buy clothes on a credit card and still run that debt after the items are out of fashion and stuck in the wardrobe unworn.

Good debt can be buying something that you could not buy out of income: you need a new cooker or washing machine, you need a car, your daughter is getting married. These amounts can be hard to find without debt and, of course, they have to be paid for now rather than in a few years' time. Those debts can run for a couple of years, maybe three; but if you have to run them much beyond that it probably means you could not afford the item in the first place.

Finally, there is the new kitchen or bathroom, the loft extension or the new garage. Improvements to your home can be paid back over a longer period and the debt can be secured on your home. In other words, if you find you cannot repay the debt then your home is at risk. You should avoid that if you can but home improvements (in moderation) are probably the one kind of debt that is worth securing on your home.

MORTGAGES

Borrowing money to buy a property used to be simple. Interest rates were more or less fixed, deposits were fairly standard, and you could borrow a fixed multiple of your annual salary. You paid off the interest and the capital and at the end of the 25 years, your home was yours. Not any more.

If you are still in one of those contracts you are probably wasting money. Most of us stick with the same mortgage we have had since we bought our home; but that can be a very expensive mistake. Many homeowners are wasting thousands of pounds by doing nothing. Many of them are people who took out their loan when the mortgage market was very different. So a very important thing to do in your 50s is check your mortgage and see if you can save money on it. After all, every penny saved now is another tuppence in your retirement. Even if the mortgage you have now is expensive, check the penalty clauses before you change to another, however.

Mortgages in the UK have never been so competitive. Every bank and building society wants our business and so they make good offers to get new customers. The choice can seem bewildering. Don't let that put you off. Just look at the figures. If you have a £50,000 loan and you're paying the standard sort of interest rate (which is around 6 per cent), then there are risk-free deals around that will save you £95 a month (more than £1,100 a year). That saving applies to people who have an interest-only mortgage that you will repay with an endowment or from some other capital at the end. A repayment mortgage will save you less but the savings are still considerable. If your mortgage is twice as big, the savings are doubled.

Be aware, however, that as you get older lenders get more reluctant to lend. If you are an employee, you will not normally be allowed to take on a mortgage beyond the age of 65, and if you are self-employed the limit is usually 70. To get a mortgage lasting beyond those ages you have to show that you will have the income from a pension or other sources to meet the repayments. It is also important to make sure that you are happy you can afford the repayments as you get older.

Types of mortgage

You have to decide which sort of mortgage to go for. Most mortgages are what is called 'variable rate'. In other words, as the Bank of England changes the bank rate, so your mortgage rate will go up and down. All lenders have what they call a standard variable rate (SVR) – this is the sort of benchmark mortgage typically a couple of percentage points above the base rate. Anyone paying that standard variable rate is wasting money.

Fixed rate mortgages fix the rate of interest for a period of time. It can be for at least two years, although some will fix for five, and you can get deals fixed for longer. The advantage of a fixed rate deal is that you know what your payments will be for the fixed period, and if interest rates rise you will be protected against extra costs. Of course, if rates fall then you will end up paying more. You will also have to be aware of when the fixed rate ends and be prepared to move your mortgage again then. Always make sure with a fixed rate that there are no penalties if you switch to another lender once the fixed rate runs out; that leaves you free to move your mortgage again in a few years.

Discounted rate mortgages guarantee that the rate you are charged will be a fixed amount below the lender's standard rate for a mortgage. For example, if the standard variable rate is 6 per cent, a discount may offer up to 2.5 per cent off that for a fixed period of two years.

There are several other variations on these themes. With **capped rate mortgages**, lenders offer a mortgage that will go down when rates fall, but any increase will stop at a certain level – the cap. They may seem like a one-way bet, but in fact you will not get such a good deal at first as one of the more straightforward products. Essentially you have to decide if you want fixed or variable. Doing nothing –

sticking with what you've got without shopping around – is not really an option unless you want to waste money.

Flexible deals

Once you have chosen fixed or variable for your rate, then you should also check if the mortgage is what is called 'flexible'. In the past, you made the monthly repayments and that was that. If you came into some money, you could be penalised for paying extra off your loan. If you lost your job, the only sympathy if you missed a payment would be a threatening letter. Now, things can be different.

Flexible mortgages allow you to miss payments, increase or decrease them or pay a lump sum off the loan – and then borrow it back later if you need it. Flexible mortgages are a very useful financial planning tool. They enable you to save up money by paying down your mortgage debt and then borrow it off yourself later to buy something or meet a crisis. You should also check that interest is calculated on a daily basis. On older contracts the interest is worked out once a year. So even if you pay money off the loan, you get no reduction in the interest charged until the lender does its books at the year end.

The cost of changing

People are put off changing their mortgage by not knowing how to do it, or worrying that they will not really save money and fearing that the cost of changing will wipe out the savings.

There are four charges you may face:

- **Valuation** – the lender will want to make sure that your property is worth more than the loan.
- **Solicitor** – there will be some legal documents to deal with.

- **Arrangement** – some lenders charge you a fee for arranging the loan: a real cheek (it's like a supermarket charging you a fee for arranging to put the food on the shelves).
- **Broker** – you may choose to pay a broker for advising and sorting out the deal.

Reckon on up to £300 for *each* of the first three of these costs. Many lenders will not charge an arrangement fee and some will offer to pay for the valuation or legal fees up to a certain amount. Those offers are particularly valuable and may tip the balance between one deal and another that seems to offer a slightly better interest rate.

As for brokers, most will charge you a fee – some up to 1 per cent of the amount of the loan. That too is a bit of a cheek really, as they also get paid by the lender when the mortgage deal is done. So by charging you, they are being paid twice for the same job. It is also important to make sure that the broker you go to is part of a national and respected chain. Some brokers are unscrupulous and will put your loan with an unsuitable lender.

You can compare all mortgage products at www.moneyfacts.co.uk

From 31 October 2004 mortgage brokers will have to be registered with the Financial Services Authority and you will be able to seek compensation if you feel they have mis-sold you a product that was not suitable for you. The FSA produces comparisons of mortgage products on its website at www.fsa.gov.uk/tables

Endowments

One of the big financial scandals of the last 20 years is the mis-selling of endowment mortgages. Many people now in their 50s were targeted by sales staff mainly working for big insurance companies, and many are now finding that the promises they were made will not be kept.

An endowment mortgage is two products. First, you have a mortgage on which you only pay the interest on the loan. So after 25 years you still owe as much as you did at the start. Second, you pay monthly into an investment called an endowment. Your money is invested on the stock market, usually in a 'with profits' fund (see page 22) and a small part of your monthly payment also goes to buy life insurance so that if you die during the period of the loan your debt is paid off.

The problem with this deal is that it links a fixed amount of debt which has to be repaid at a fixed time to an uncertain investment, the value of which depends on the growth in a fund which is mainly invested in the stock market. So there is a risk that at the time you need it, the investment will be too little to repay the loan. It is a risk that insurance companies and sales representatives almost never explained. Projections were made on a high basis, and the fall in the stock market since has meant that, for many people, it is now almost impossible that they will get the returns needed to catch up in time to pay off the mortgage. The latest estimate from the Financial Services Authority is that three and a half million homeowners have a mortgage linked to an endowment which will not repay the loan when it falls due. They face an average shortfall of £8,250 – a total shortfall approaching £30 billion.

Will it be enough?

More than seven out of ten endowments will probably not be enough to repay the loan they are linked to. If you are in that position you will have had a letter from your endowment provider warning you of this. It is very important that you take action. But it is not always easy to work out what to do. One thing you should never do is increase the payments on your endowment – that is simply throwing good money after bad. The most important thing is to restructure your mortgage so that come what may your endowment will repay it. If you have not re-mortgaged already you should do that. But instead of taking the cut in your monthly payments and spending it, carry on paying at the same rate. In that way you will reduce your debt. If everyone had done that as interest rates fell, there would not be an endowment crisis now.

You could convert the loan to a repayment mortgage. If you can afford to do it, that may be the best thing to do – at least you will know that your mortgage will be repaid.

You can reduce the cost of doing that by either selling or cashing in your endowment policy. That will almost certainly produce a disappointing amount. But if you use it to reduce your mortgage and divert the payments you were making to paying your loan as well, you may find that you will have enough to be sure that your loan will be repaid at the end.

If you do consider selling or paying off your endowment and you have a partner or dependants, remember to take out life insurance to cover the loan if you die before it is repaid. Even if you do not have a partner or dependants, the lender may insist on life cover.

An alternative to cashing in or selling your endowment is to make it what is called 'paid up'. You keep the investment fund but do not add any more to it over the years. Divert those monthly payments to repaying your mortgage, add as much more as you can and then you may also find that when the loan comes to its end, the paid-up endowment is sufficient to cover it. This solution can often be the best.

If you are anticipating that the endowment will not repay your loan and the maturity date is around your retirement age, you may well feel that there is too little time left to take action. In that case you have to consider how to repay the debt. One way is to use any lump sum you may be expecting from a pension plan or from redundancy. That may not be how you anticipated using it, but it is a practical use for the money when faced with a debt as you reach retirement.

Alternatively, you could take out a short-term loan secured on the property which you could afford to repay out of your pension. This course of action would ensure that you finally did own all of your home before reaching too great an age. Of course, you could sell the place and buy somewhere cheaper with the balance of the money after paying off the shortfall on your mortgage (see pages 177–181 for information about trading down).

Another alternative is to ask a member of your family who was anticipating inheriting your home to meet the shortfall. Remember, however, that if you continue to live there, the whole value of the property will count as part of your estate when it comes to working out Inheritance Tax.

If all else fails, you could consider taking out what is called a 'lifetime mortgage' to cover the existing loan. At 60 you would be able to borrow up to 25 per cent of the value of your home, which will probably be enough to meet the shortfall on the endowment. These lifetime mortgages are the same as equity release roll-up loans (see pages 181–182). Make sure that you get one with a guarantee that the loan plus rolled-up interest will never exceed the value of the property – called a 'no negative equity guarantee'. Make sure too that your heirs know what you are doing; otherwise they may be very disappointed when you finally die to discover that an insurance company owns your home.

Mis-selling

Just because your endowment is not now on track to meet your mortgage does not mean you were mis-sold it. However, the Consumers' Association estimates that even more people were mis-sold than have a shortfall – around five million. Most people with endowments believe two things. Firstly, they were told that the endowment 'would' pay off the mortgage. Secondly, they were told that the endowment 'would probably' be more than was needed to repay the mortgage, leaving them with a tax-free sum to spend. If you think about it, anyone who was honestly told that the product might produce a surplus but might also fail to repay the debt would probably not have taken one on.

Being told that your endowment 'would' pay off the mortgage was undoubtedly a mis-sale. It is hard to prove, however, because the insurance companies were very careful never to put such things in writing. Whatever the salesperson may have told you – and, to be fair, probably believed – the company would make sure it was protected by the small print in the documents you were sent. You should also have been told about the alternatives, and the risk you took should have been explained to you. But, again, if you were not it is hard to prove as most of the sales process, particularly in the early days, was by word of mouth.

Other things are easier to prove. If the repayments on your endowment took you beyond your expected retirement age, then you were almost certainly mis-sold the product. If you had an existing endowment and you were persuaded to cash it in and sold a replacement, that was certainly a mis-sale.

Even if you were mis-sold you may not be able to get redress. If your product was sold to you in 1988 or earlier you may be blocked.

If you have a mortgage linked to an endowment, check the Consumers' Association website at www.endowmentaction.co.uk which explains mis-sales, how to get redress, and will even generate a letter for you to send to start the complaint process. It also explains the options if you face a shortfall.

CREDIT CARDS

Credit cards are a fantastic invention. They are a wonderful way to manage money in the short term: but they are a terrible way to take on debt in the long term. Used carefully they are a financial planning aid: used foolishly they pave the road to ruin.

Like many other financial products there is tremendous competition among credit card providers. They want your business and there are special deals for new customers that are very good news. You can pay nothing for debt for nine months; you can pay a low rate of interest until the debt is paid off; or you can get paid every time you use your card. You cannot get all this at once, however. You must play the market and remember the first rule of financial services in the 21st Century – loyalty is punished, disloyalty is rewarded.

If you have credit or store cards you should check what deal you are getting. Whether you run up debts or pay it all off at once, you could lose out if you do not play the field and swap cards from time to time. You have to be well-organised with all these deals, however, and make sure that you don't lose track of what you are doing and when you must change. If you are not well-organised, don't do anything which relies on getting the timing spot on.

Short-term debt

If you do not pay off your card in full each month, then you should make sure you are not paying through the nose. Store cards can charge you 30 per cent a year for borrowing money. In other words, if you have £1,000 credit on the card it will cost you £300 a year (£6 a week). Even if you pay it off in a regular manner, you will end up paying £150 for the privilege of borrowing it. Credit cards that are not linked to a particular store or chain are better – but at their worst you can be paying more than 20 per cent on your debt. Few charge less than 10 per cent and even the best will charge you 8 per cent, which is twice the Bank of England base rate. These rates are alright for short-term debt – a few months to spread the load of buying something you need or want – but they are not good if you allow the debt to linger longer.

Long-term debt

Although credit cards are generally a mistake for long-term debt, you can find long-term debt deals that are really worth having. Many cards allow new customers to transfer debt – either from another card or from a bank overdraft – to that card. Suppose you have £5,000 of debt on other cards that you really cannot see your way to paying. You can find a card that offers you a fixed rate for the life of the debt. They are called 'life of balance' deals and they mean that the debt is charged at a low rate until it is paid off. At the time of writing you can get less than 4 per cent on life of balance deals. Pay the minimum each month and you can watch the debt run down. It will take around 13 years to repay it but for all that time the interest rates are low.

If you have a debt that you can pay off in a shorter time than that, then consider a zero per cent card. They will charge you nothing for your debt, typically for six months, but if you search you can find nine months. Ideally, divide your debt by the number of months and pay it off over that period. Alternatively, you can take out another card at the end of the time. But do not just put the debt off hoping something will turn up – make sure you have a plan to pay it off.

At the end of these special deals the interest rate will revert to the high levels that credit card companies normally charge, usually in double figures. Some cards have another trick up their sleeve too. Although they guarantee the interest rate on the debt you transfer, they do not make the same offer on new debt. So if you buy things with the card, they will charge you a high rate on those purchases and any payment you make is taken off the low interest rate debt first. So you find you are clocking up more interest than you expect. If you take out a low interest credit card for debt, do not use it for purchases or you might get stung. Always check the small print.

Money back

Credit cards can be financially useful for people without debt too. If you pay off your card in full each month, you pay no interest. Some cards will pay you each time you use them. These are called 'cashback' cards and every time you use the card to buy something the company will credit you with, normally, half a per cent of what you spend. Some will credit you with more – one per cent is the highest you can get but those deals are few and far between and do not usually last very long. The card companies can afford it because they charge the retailer every time you use the card (typically 2.5 per cent). So by encouraging you to use the card more, they make more money, a small part of which they share with you. Money back is a good offer. Loyalty points, air miles, and all the other schemes which seem to give you advantages from using the card are not really worth having, however.

The best website for information on good credit card deals is www.moneysavingexpert.com You can also find deals that are not available elsewhere, as well as a lot of comparative information, at www.moneysupermarket.com

BANK LOANS

If you want to borrow money to buy something expensive that you cannot afford out of your monthly income, then a loan from the bank can be the best way to get it. Bank loans tend to be over a fixed period from one to five years. Over that time you pay a fixed amount each month, and at the end the debt is paid off. If you repay the loan early you can get hit with penalties, so they are inflexible. The rate of interest is fixed, however, so you know how much it will cost you.

Never borrow money to buy something for longer than it will last; so don't take out a two-year bank loan to pay for an annual holiday. Never take out repayment insurance either as it can double the cost of the interest on the loan. In many cases it will not pay out even if you lose your job and find you cannot meet the repayments. It is almost always a waste of precious income.

Bank loans vary greatly in their cost. Your own bank will seldom be the cheapest place to borrow money. If you have internet access, you can borrow money at less than 6 per cent; on the high street you can pay double that easily.

At some point most of us have let our current account slip into an overdraft. They are usually not a cheap way to borrow, although they are very flexible. It is never a good idea to borrow for more than a few days through an overdraft. It is certainly never wise to do so if you do not have an agreement to go overdrawn; the rate charged then will be usurious.

APR

When you are comparing credit cards or other loans you will see a percentage called an Annual Percentage Rate (APR). The APR is supposed to be a standard way of calculating the interest charged on a loan so that you can make fair comparisons. However, banks and other lenders have made such comparisons almost impossible by finding ways to bend the rules. The Consumers' Association has calculated that there are now ten different ways used by card providers to work out the monthly repayment on a credit card. It claims that a single purchase of £300 on a card that charges interest at an APR of 18.9 per cent can lead to a monthly charge for interest ranging from £5.50 to £9.54. The Government is currently looking at APR and how it is worked out. Meanwhile all credit card providers have agreed to produce a single 'summary box' in plain English and in a common format that shows the main terms of their cards.

However, one particular problem will not be solved by that box and has actually been caused by the Office of Fair Trading (OFT) itself. In the past, cards tempted us with offers of '0 per cent APR for six months'. But the OFT decided that is misleading – APR is an Annual Percentage Rate, so quoting it over half a year is wrong. Cards that offer a lower interest rate for the first six months and then a higher rate after that now have to declare what is called a 'blended rate' on their card. The trouble is that there is not one way of working out this blended rate. The OFT says the method used should take account of the time taken to repay the debt on the card over the maximum period. So, for example, a card with a six month 0 per cent offer followed by a rate of 16.9 per cent would be shown under OFT rules as an APR of 13.9 per cent – a rate no-one pays at any time. It is much more important to check how long the 0 per cent offer lasts and what the rate is after it has finished. These problems have yet to be resolved. Meanwhile, take care.

BAD DEBT

If your income falls or your expenses rise for some reason, credit is so easy to get nowadays that you can easily get into debt. The golden rule with debt is never ignore it. If you do, it will not go away; it will just get worse. Creditors would rather hear bad news from you than nothing at all.

There are some simple steps to take with debt. First, get out and put into order all the bits of paper relating to your debts. If some have been thrown away, use what are left; and get a copy of the missing ones or fill in the details by hand.

Second, write down what you owe and put the debts in priority order – first the debts that have to be paid:

- **Mortgage** – because you have to live somewhere
- **Other debt secured on your home** – because if you do not pay that your home is at risk
- **Rent** – because you don't want to be evicted
- **Council Tax** – because you can be jailed if you do not pay it
- **Electricity or gas bills** – because they can disconnect you if you do not pay
- **Any debts where court action is being threatened** – you cannot normally be jailed for debt but getting what is called a County Court judgement against you should be avoided if possible.

Then look at your commercial debts – credit cards, bank loans, hire purchase agreements, and anything that is not related to where you live. Write down the debts that have the highest rates of interest: if you do not know which they are, that is part of your problem. Find out. It will be on a piece of paper somewhere.

Then look at your income. Write down what you have coming in each month. Write down too what you have to pay out each month regularly – rent or mortgage, electricity and gas, telephone, fares to work, and food – although make sure you only include essentials here, not meals out, takeaways, or chocolate.

The difference, if positive, is what you can afford to use to begin to pay off your debts. Start with the priorities – things you have to pay to keep yourself secure in your home – then go on to what can you afford to pay off to reduce the debts that have the highest rates of interest.

If you feel the problem is too big for you to deal with, then get help. There are organisations that will help you with your debt and negotiate with your creditors so they defer repayments or accept small steps towards repaying the loan. Sometimes they will even manage to get debts written off. Although these organisations are under a lot of pressure and it may not be possible to get a face-to-face interview, you can at least talk problems through on the phone, and get a 'kit' to help with drawing up budgets and model letters etc. Whatever you do, never pay anyone to help you. There are many companies around that will offer help for a fee. If you already owe too much money, the last thing you need to do is spend money on something else.

You can contact the Consumer Credit Counselling Service on Freephone 0800 138 1111 (www.cccs.co.uk); National Debtline on 0808 808 4000 (www.nationaldebtline.co.uk); or your local Citizens Advice Bureau. You can find the address for your local CAB at www.citizensadvice.org.uk or in the phone book.

Consolidation

However bad your debt, never consider consolidating it through one of the many companies around that offer to do that. Although they will seem to reduce your monthly outgoings they will do that in two ways. First, they will push your debt into the future by lending you money over five or ten years or even longer. Of course, that reduces your immediate outgoings but it means that you are committed to paying the debt off for very many years and paying large amounts of interest. Second, they will secure the debt on your home – in other words it is like a second mortgage. If you miss payments, then ultimately they can make you sell your home to pay them back. The rates they charge are extortionate and they are never a good idea.

However, it can be worth getting a personal loan from your bank to pay off high-interest credit card or store card debt – as long as you can trust yourself not to start running up a new series of debts once you have done so. Cut up your cards if you can't be sure of that.

Age

Lenders do not normally discriminate against people in their 50s when it comes to lending money. They will credit score you, of course (see below), and they will want to be sure that your retirement will not interfere with your ability to meet the repayments.

Credit scoring

When you apply for a loan or a credit card, the lender will put your details through a process which is called credit scoring. Each lender has different rules but they all use a common database of information provided by three credit reference companies. They collect information from banks, building societies, and utility companies about how regularly you pay your bills, noting in particular whether you have overdue payments. Information is also stored about the number of credit searches made on your file. Having a lot of searches may count against you. They also collect publicly available information from the electoral register to check that you live where you say you do, and from the court information system about judgments for debt that may have been made against you, and, of course, information about bankruptcy.

The lender will apply its own rules to all this information and either accept or reject your application. Of course, having judgements against you for debt or being a habitual late payer will tend to move you to the 'rejected' pile. But in theory you may still be able to get credit from some lender at some price. More and more lenders now use what they call 'risk pricing'. In other words, the greater the risk you pose, the higher the interest rate you will be charged. At the time of writing, Barclaycard, for example, charges its customers interest ranging from 11.9 per cent to 24.9 per cent, depending on how big a risk the lender deems you to be. Once you have taken out the card and paid regularly, you can ask to be moved to a lower rate of interest.

Although the rules lenders use are kept a closely guarded secret, you can see the file of information they use. All you need do is apply to the credit reference companies and ask for a copy of your file. There are two major companies – Experian and Equifax – and a newcomer called Call Credit. They are legally obliged to send you a copy and are only allowed to charge £2. You can apply by post or online using a debit or credit card. Both companies will offer you more services at a higher cost, but for your statutory copy of your own credit record they can only charge £2. Equifax in particular makes it seem that you have to pay £8.25. You do not.

Credit repair

If you are turned down for credit, the first thing to do is ask the lender. It should tell you the main reason for declining you but it may not be very informative. You can also get your credit record from the credit reference agencies. If there is a mistake on it, then you can get that corrected by applying to the credit reference agency. The problem is that most of the information they use comes from other sources, so you will end up having to get the bank or court which provided the information to correct their records and then pass that on to the credit reference agencies. It can be a difficult and time-consuming process. The credit reference agencies are very adept at passing the responsibility for the information they hold on to other people. Their websites all contain information about how to go about getting errors corrected.

If there is something which is true but you feel needs explaining, then you can add a comment of up to 200 words to your file. It is by no means certain, however, that this will help you get credit. If you are married or you share a name with someone else at the same address, then your files may be linked – if one of you is refused, others may be too. You can stop this by getting a notice of disassociation; and that is particularly important when you get divorced to ensure that your ex-spouse's credit record does not affect you.

If you are taken to court for debt and an order is made against you which you do not pay in time, the judgement – or decree in Scotland – remains on your file for six years after it is made and there is nothing you can do to get it removed, even if the debt has been paid. Some companies claim to be able to 'repair' your credit record. They cannot do more than you might be able to do free. Never use them and never pay them. If you have been declared bankrupt, that information remains on your file for six years regardless of whether you have been discharged (although the fact of your discharge will be shown when that happens).

INSURANCE

Throughout our lives we accumulate various financial products that we may not need. Life insurance, illness insurance, payment protection insurance, extended warranties, credit card protection – all sorts of things. Some of them were useless when we took them out; some will become useless with the passage of time. Your 50s is a good time to take another look at all these old deals, get rid of the ones you do not need, and concentrate your money on the ones that serve a useful purpose.

LIFE INSURANCE

Insurance salespeople tell us that life insurance is sold not bought – in other words, if they did not point out the advantages no-one would bother to insure their life. They also tell us that we have far too little life insurance or 'cover' as they like to call it. One insurance company estimates that we are £2 billion under-insured on life cover. But is it true? Many of us accumulate life insurance which is indeed sold – not openly but as part of our pension, our endowment, our mortgage, or with other insurance such as protection against illness or unemployment.

In your 50s you may have several lots of life cover that you are paying for. You should consider getting rid of it if you do not need it. The first thing to check is your company pension scheme. If you belong to one – especially one in which the pension is related to your salary – you will almost certainly have life cover, of up to three or even four times your annual gross pay. That can be more than enough for most people, although, of course, you will lose that if you leave your job, and it may be lost or reduced on retirement.

The second thing to ask is – do you have dependants? If not, what do you need life insurance for? In our 50s we may acquire new dependants – parents, aunts or uncles, brothers or sisters, or, of course, partners or spouses or step-children. But in each case it is important to ask if they will need money if you die – and if not, why should you pay for a product to give them something they will not need?

Once you reach your 50s, your children, if you have them, will often be relatively independent. When they are young and dependent on you and your death would leave them without a home, an education, or all those things you spend on them, then life cover is a good idea – if you do not already have it from your job or your pension scheme. It is usually called 'term assurance' and it runs out once your youngest child reaches a certain age (usually around 21 when they have finished university). If you have taken out life insurance in the past with a view to protecting dependent children, consider cancelling it if they are no longer dependent.

If you have a mortgage – particularly an interest-only mortgage – and you share your home with a partner or someone else, then you should have life insurance to make sure that the property becomes theirs when you die. You do not want to leave anyone with the worry of homelessness or paying off a mortgage. But make sure that the sum assured will not form part of your estate. If it does and you leave more than £263,000 altogether, then the Chancellor could snaffle 40 per cent of this amount in Inheritance Tax. The way round this is to get the policy written in trust so that the money is not part of your estate but is left to trustees – normally the insurance company – which will then pass it on for the purpose you state. You can arrange this when you take the insurance out, or later – ask the insurance company. (See pages 78–81 for more about Inheritance Tax.)

Apart from dependent children and your home, the only other reason to have life insurance is to provide for your partner or someone else who is financially dependent on you. In that case if you die before you expect they will lose the share of your income they are used to benefiting from. But you have to ask yourself whether they really are dependent on your income? How much of it genuinely goes to their benefit and not yours? If you die what will they really need?

One company has recently started marketing life insurance for people in their 50s so that debts are cleared on death. This bizarre product is supposed to offer your heirs peace of mind. But from what? When you die, your estate is added up – all your assets on one side and any debts on the other. The debts are paid from your estate. If there is not enough – in other words your debts were bigger than your assets – then your debts are written off by the companies. They cannot chase your heirs for your debt after your death.

Cancelling unnecessary life cover can save you money. The unnecessary sale of life cover comes back to commission – the sales agent can get more than two year's premiums upfront and 2½ per cent of your annual premiums thereafter.

ILLNESS AND DISABILITY

When you take out life insurance you will also frequently be offered other forms of insurance. What if you do not die but have a dread disease such as cancer, stroke or heart disease?

Critical illness cover

Critical illness cover has become very fashionable with financial advisers recently. A million policies were sold in 2002 alone and more than five million of us have this cover – usually sold with other products such as life cover, and especially targeted at home buyers and self-employed people. It costs around £30 a month and typically pays out around £100,000 if you get one of seven 'dread diseases', perhaps enabling you at least to pay off your mortgage.

Sales of these policies depend on our fear of getting one of these so-called 'dread diseases'. With more people living longer, more of us will get them and survive them. As a result insurers are stepping up the criteria for making a claim. Some policies may only pay out after your second heart bypass operation, for example, and some cancers are being excluded from claims. Premiums are also rising. In April 2003 one company raised the cost of its critical illness insurance by 70 per cent, even for 50,000 people who had signed up before the price rise! So it is more than probable that over the next few years these policies will become prohibitively expensive and the conditions for claiming will be tightened further. In other words, just when you need it you will find that the premiums you have paid for many years were a waste of money.

Commission rates, of course, are high – about ten times as high as commission on disability insurance which covers conditions we are all much more likely to suffer from. You should only consider it if you really like your financial adviser.

Permanent health insurance

Permanent health insurance (PHI) is a better bet. (It is also called 'total permanent disability cover' or sometimes 'income protection'.) It pays out to replace income if a disability or illness means you cannot work – or carry on with your self-employment. Low commission rates mean that it is not so popular with advisers. However, the odds are higher that you will get a disabling rather than a life-threatening illness.

You can cover up to 75 per cent of your earnings, although some insurers will now only cover up to 60 per cent. The policy will pay out if you are incapable of doing any work, not just the job you normally do – that is a pretty tough criterion to meet. You can reduce the premiums by lengthening the delay between the disability and the pay out; you can choose between about four weeks and two years. Inevitably as you get older the premiums become more expensive; in your 50s often prohibitively so.

BAD INSURANCE

There are other insurance products that are almost always a waste of money.

Credit card protection

If you lose your credit cards, you are not responsible for the debts run up by the thieves as long as you report the theft or loss to the credit card company swiftly. So all you need to do is remember the cards you have and take the helpline numbers with you when you are on holiday.

Extended warranties

Extended warranties are nothing of the kind. They are a form of breakdown insurance. Retail laws ensure that if something goes wrong in the first 12 months you can usually get your money back from the retailer and most goods have a warranty of at least a year from the manufacturer. Some stores guarantee products for longer. Research by the Consumers' Association has shown that modern appliances are generally reliable beyond the time the breakdown insurance lasts. So it is generally a waste of money. Sales staff in the shop earn commission for selling it and the retailers often make much of their profit from it. Just say 'no'. Unfortunately, these insurance products sold by retailers at the point of sale will not be regulated by the Financial Services Authority when it takes over almost all other general insurance in January 2005.

Payment protection cover

When you take out a loan, a credit card, hire purchase, or a mortgage you will usually be asked if you want to take out insurance as well to protect your payments if you should lose your job or fall ill and be unable to meet the repayments. The correct answer is 'no'. These policies have many exclusions – not least for self-employed people and, of course, those who do not have paid work – and do not cover losing your job through redundancy or your own fault. The period of cover is often very short and the cost is high. With a bank loan, for example, the cost of the payment protection insurance can be as high or highor than the total cost of the interest on the loan.

Private health insurance

In the UK we are fortunate to have a high quality free health care service paid for out of taxation. Yes there are problems, yes there can be delays, but ultimately you get cured free. So when you weigh up the cost of private health care, remember you are not buying the cost of private medical care – you are buying the cost of the advantage over the NHS. You are buying a private room, a shorter wait, perhaps more personal treatment; but the chances are the actual medical care will be by the same people who would have given it to you on the NHS.

As we get older the chances of needing medical care grow and the cost of private medical insurance grows too. So do not fall into the trap of paying the premiums when you are young only to find you cannot afford them in your late 50s just as you approach the time that you are more likely to make a claim.

One way of paying for medical care is to keep some money, a few thousand pounds if you can afford it, in a separate account earning interest against the time when you may need medical treatment that the NHS will not do or will not do quickly enough. People who need a hip replacement, for example, may be in severe pain and have little mobility, but the operation is not a priority for the NHS and the wait can be very long. Paying privately might be a sensible option to cut that time.

The big private hospital groups now offer fixed price deals for common operations, which include the fees, drugs, investigations, the operation itself, and time in hospital to recover. The fee covers the whole package and if there are complications you do not pay for them. Prices for these deals vary widely but cataract removal or treatment for varicose veins or a hernia can cost around £2,000. If you need a hip replaced expect to pay about £8,000, or around £10,000 for a knee. Sometimes you can get a better deal by going abroad. If you cannot afford to save this sort of money, then you could perhaps borrow it against the value of your home. Either way it can be a lot cheaper than paying the growing cost of private health care premiums as you move through your 50s. A lot of those costs are for expensive heart operations or extended cancer treatments when those are realistically better done on the NHS.

For more on the cost of common operations and medical insurance, phone Care Health on 01494 680202 or see its website at www.carehealth.co.uk

Care home fees

The market for insurance against the cost of care in a care home is a relatively new one. As with private medical care, think carefully what you are actually buying. The great majority of us – about four out of five – never need to go into a care home; we die in our own homes or in a hospital.

Remember too that you may be able to get help from the State:

- the NHS is currently responsible for the full costs of your care if you need full-time nursing care;
- if you cannot get full help, the NHS makes a contribution towards the cost of nursing care; and
- if you have savings of less than £20,000 (in England in 2004–2005), then the local council will help towards the fees in a care home.

Many people are afraid that they will have to sell their home to pay for their care. However, if your spouse or partner is still living there then the value of your home is ignored. It is also ignored if a relative who is over 60 or is disabled lives there. Even if the value of your home is not ignored – if it is empty for example – then you do not have to sell it. You can do a deal with the local council called a 'deferred payment agreement' whereby the council pays the part of the fees you cannot and you in effect run up a debt to the council for that amount. No interest is charged on it. When you die the debt is repaid from your estate. Meanwhile your home can be let out if you want, and you benefit from the rising value of your property for the rest of your life. The chances are that the debt will be quite small compared to the value of your home and your heirs will not suffer that much disadvantage. So deferred payment may be an option – you will need to get financial advice about the best thing to do in your circumstances.

So when you consider insuring against the cost of care home fees, remember three things:

- There is a five to one chance you will never need to go into a home.
- Even if you do, you may get help with the fees.

- Even if you do not get help, you should not have to sell your home to pay for it (although there is a chance that some of the value of your home will have to be used to pay for your care).

For these reasons, insurance to pay for the cost of long-term care is seldom useful. However, some people may want to consider it. In particular, if you are paying for yourself – either through insurance or by using the proceeds of your home – you will get more choice over the home you stay in and the quality of the living accommodation you get. A room of your own, a home that you like, or simply being in an area you are familiar with, will all be much more possible if you do not have to rely on the State. Some people may pay for insurance simply to give them peace of mind (although that may disappear when you actually try to claim on it). Others will choose it because they want to guarantee that they preserve the family home in full for their heirs.

Many people in their 50s consider arranging their affairs so that their home cannot be taken into account at all for paying care home fees. It is seen as a form of tax planning, like giving property away to reduce Inheritance Tax. But the rules that apply to IHT (see pages 78–81) are completely different from those that apply to the means test for care home fees. One obvious solution that many people come up with is to give their home away and continue to live in it. If you do not own it, they think, no-one can touch it. That is not always true. The rules are complex and if you make a mistake you – or your relatives – could end up in difficulties.

There are two sorts of long-term care insurance:

- **Immediate care plans** – you buy one if you have reached the stage where you have been assessed as needing care and you have to find a way to pay for it. You pay a lump sum and you get an annual sum to pay towards your care.

■ **Monthly premium plans** – you start paying into one before you need care – perhaps in your 50s – and if your health deteriorates so that you do need care, the plan will pay up to a specified amount each year.

In either case you will not normally get a guarantee to get all your fees paid; just the balance you need on top of your pensions and any other income.

The cost of monthly premiums will depend on your age and sex and some companies will expect a medical history.

The plan will pay out once you find it impossible to do two or three daily living tasks including preparing food, using the toilet, washing, dressing and so on.

If you want to spend money on long-term care insurance, make sure you are clear what guarantees the plan gives.

The rules about care home fees and who pays what are hidoously complex, different in England, Wales, Scotland and Northern Ireland, and are liable to change as policy is adjusted and the courts decide exactly what the laws mean. It is vital to get advice. Age Concern has a series of factsheets about the rules – you can find them on the website at www.ageconcern.org.uk or call the Age Concern Information Line on 0800 00 99 66.

| GOOD INSURANCE |

One great advantage of growing older is that we become a better risk financially. We pay our debts, don't get overextended, and take care of our property. So insurance companies like us and will offer better deals just because of our age. We also tick other boxes – we often own our own home without, or with a low, mortgage; we have probably lived at the same address for a long time; we have fewer dependants and a higher income. They love us. That means it can be cheaper to insure our car, our home and its contents.

Don't get seduced by offers that are just for the over 50s, however. You can often do as well if not better by using the Internet to search for the best insurance deals. The AA insurance premium index shows that the average cost of car insurance at the time of writing is £777 a year – but if you shop around you can get it for a little more than half that (£495), saving nearly £300 a year. You can save a similar percentage on insuring your buildings and contents. Remember too that if you still insure your home with your mortgage lender, you can almost always save money by insuring it with another company. Lenders can no longer insist that you take out insurance with them as a condition of the mortgage.

When you do go for bargain price insurance, make sure that it gives you the cover you want. It is not worth saving a few pounds to find that you are liable for a hefty excess if you make a claim. Also, go with a company whose name you trust.

FINANCIAL ADVICE

If you have a significant sum of money you may want to go to a financial adviser. Despite their name, most financial advisers are principally salespeople – most of them work for one company and their job is to sell you stuff. It is like calling the people who work in a hi-fi shop 'audio-visual consultants'. Some of them may be very knowledgeable but their job is to sell things. Their living – and that of their employer – depends on sales.

Major changes in the way that financial advice is structured will begin late in 2004 and there will be a six-month transition period when the old and the new systems will both be in place. While both systems are running it will be particularly difficult to get to grips with exactly what kind of adviser you are dealing with.

INDEPENDENT FINANCIAL ADVISERS

One thing will remain common between the two systems. Some people are called Independent Financial Advisers and that title 'independent' is very important. By law they have to find the most suitable product for their client after considering every single product on the market from every company in the UK. They must not work for, or have a business relationship with, any product provider. They must, in other words, be truly 'independent'. If you need financial advice you should only ever go to an Independent Financial Adviser (an IFA).

At the moment IFAs can be paid by the commission they earn on the products they sell, or by a fee you pay them, or a combination of the two. After the 2004–2005 changes they will have to be willing to be paid only by a fee. But with your agreement they can be paid by commission, by fee, or both. (There is more on commission and fees on pages 118–120.)

AGENTS

People who are not 'independent' have ties to one or more companies. In that sense their advice is not independent; they only sell the products of one or a limited number of companies. At the moment, they are normally tied to just one company – so for example Prudential agents will only sell you Prudential products. They are called, appropriately, 'tied agents'.

After the 2004–2005 changes, agents will also be able to be associated with a group of companies. So they might decide to sell insurance from three companies, unit trusts from four fund managers, and perhaps mortgages from half a dozen lenders. They will have to tell you which companies they are associated with. In the industry the jargon for them is 'multi-tied' agents – in other words tied to several companies. But in practice anyone who is registered to sell financial products and not independent will call themselves simply a 'financial adviser'.

Some will continue to be employed by one financial company, but they will still be able to offer a range of products from other companies. For example, someone may work for a high street bank, but if that bank decides to link up with a major insurance company to offer investments, then the bank will sell those through its own workforce. But the advice given will always be partial: they may advise you to buy a product even though a better one exists with a company they do not have a business relationship with. These non-independent financial advisers will be able to make their living from fees, commission, salary, or a mixture of any of them. All of them will rely on commission for at least part of their pay and many of them will rely on it for most or all of their remuneration.

NEW PROCEDURES

From 14 January 2005, all financial advisers will have to give you a document which sets out how they operate. It is formally called an 'initial disclosure document' but will probably be headed 'Key facts about our services'. It will tell you if the company deals with products from 'the whole market' – in other words that they are an IFA – or if it deals with products from a 'limited number' of companies or 'can only deal with products' from a single company. The name of that company or of the limited number of companies will appear somewhere in the document.

They will also at some point give you what is called a 'menu card' which will set out how the company is paid and what that will cost you. This menu should show the fees or the commission that the company may receive. There may also be an indication of how those charges compare to the typical market rate.

All financial advisers of any type have to follow some common rules, and these will remain much the same after the changes:

- They will have to carry out a full interview with their client and establish what their investment aims and objectives are and judge which financial products best suit the client's needs.
- All individual financial advisers and the companies or networks they work for will have to be registered with the Financial Services Authority.
- All financial advisers will have to pass exams in financial products. There are various stages of these exams, and some advisers will be better qualified than others. There are general exams and also specific ones in particular areas of financial planning such as pensions.

To confuse things further, from later in 2005, a new grade of junior salesperson will be allowed. They will be able to sell you products branded with the word 'stakeholder', which are low-cost items, without being a fully-fledged or trained financial adviser and with only a limited 'fact-find' at the start. What they are called, or how you will be able to distinguish them from trained advisers, is not clear at the moment.

COMMISSION

Commission is at the heart of the financial services industry. It has also been at the heart of every mis-selling scandal – from personal pensions (which cost the industry £13 billion to put right) to mortgage endowments (which will leave 3½ million households £30 billion short of the money they need to buy their home); from split capital investment trusts (which lost investors £6.5 billion) to precipice bonds (total losses estimated at up to £2 billion). So deep-rooted is commission that if you go direct to the company and buy the product yourself without going through an adviser, the commission is still paid – not to you but to the company. In other words it deducts it from your investment each year and simply keeps it.

There are two sorts of commission. The first is **initial commission**. Some of the payments you make in the first year or so are handed over to the financial adviser. On a pension that can mean that the first one or two month's payments go straight to the adviser, not into your pension. For life assurance all your premiums for the first two years can go straight back to the adviser. Initial commission is normally shown on the documents you get when you sign up to the product, but normally right at the last stage (often after you have agreed to the deal). From 2005, the menu will set out the rates of commission earned.

Renewal (or trail) commission is less well known. This amount is paid each and every year to the adviser for as long as the product lasts. On a pension, for example, your adviser may get a percentage of your annual contributions into the pension. Or they may choose to have a smaller percentage of your pension fund paid to them every year. As your fund grows, so does their commission. These renewal commissions are normally paid from the annual management charges and may not be specifically mentioned in the documents you get, although the total amount of commission, and its effect on your investment, will be shown. That is why most people do not know about them. A bigger annual management charge often means a bigger annual commission paid to your adviser. Typically it is around 0.5 per cent of the value of your investment.

These annual amounts are supposed to fulfil two purposes. Firstly, they are only paid as long as you continue to pay into the product. So it discourages advisers from selling you products that are not suitable and which you will ditch. Secondly, the continuing remuneration should encourage the adviser to keep an eye on your case and to talk to you each year to make sure your investments are fulfilling your objectives. But there is no mechanism for enforcing this – it is left up to the goodwill and ethics of the adviser.

Commission is the one factor that limits the independence even of Independent Financial Advisers. The word 'independent' means that they are obliged by law to find you the best deal for your circumstances. But most IFAs earn their money by taking commission on the final sale. If they sell you nothing, they earn nothing. How much they earn depends on what they sell you, and some products are far more profitable than others. Under the law, the commission they might earn plays no part in the advice IFAs give; but human nature being what it is, customers certainly feel it does and that view is backed by research done by the Financial Services Authority.

A growing number of IFAs do not take commission; they charge their customers a fee instead. After the 2005 changes all advisers that call themselves independent will have to offer you the facility of paying fees instead of being paid through the commission on products you buy. Commission is so deep-seated in the financial services industry, however, that even they will still be paid commission by the company selling the product. So these IFAs give it back to the customer, either by increasing the size of their investment or by deducting it from their bill. At the moment some only give back the initial commission: they keep the annual commission.

All financial advisers, including those who charge a fee, should give you one free session to see if both sides think it is worth pursuing matters. Once you get into paid time, fee-paid advisers will charge an absolute minimum of £100 an hour and it will be higher – often much higher – in cities and wealthier parts of the UK. The fee will have to be paid whether you buy a product or not. If you go with commission, the adviser will not be paid unless you buy a product that pays commission.

From the first quarter of 2005 all regulated companies will have to give a clear document right at the start to show you how they are paid – fee or commission or a combination – and how much those charges are. In the case of commission, they will have to compare what they charge with average charges. These documents will lead to much greater openness and understanding of how commission works and may lead to its reduction.

CHOOSING AN IFA

It is illegal for anyone to offer financial advice on most products or to sell investments without being registered to do so. So only ever go to a registered financial adviser. If you buy financial products from a person or company that is not registered, then you are not covered by any legal protection or any compensation scheme if things go wrong.

You can check if a person or company is registered on the FSA website (www.fsa.gov.uk) or by phoning the FSA on 0845 606 1234. Always do that before dealing with someone.

The best way to find a financial adviser is by a personal recommendation from a friend who has one they trust and who has done well for them over a period of time. Remember, however, that even someone who is trusted by a friend may not be a good adviser for you, or the friend may simply be wrong and have put their faith in someone incompetent.

You can get a list of IFAs in your local area from the Internet at www.unbiased.co.uk or www.sofa.org or www.searchifa.co.uk or you can ring IFA Promotion on 0800 085 3250.

Try out two or three advisers – the first interview is free – to see if you warm to them and like what they say and their approach. Your first meeting should always be at their office, even though they may be keen to come to your home. You are more in control if you visit them. Do not be afraid to ask:

- what experience and qualifications they have;
- whether they specialise in any particular areas, such as pensions or advice for the over-50s, and what qualifications they have to do that; and
- how does the firm keep up to date with new products and developments?

You can also ask to speak to some of the firm's existing clients. If they resist that, then walk away. If they allow it, speak to the clients they offer and see how you feel about them. Finance is a very personal business and it is essential that you like and trust the people you deal with.

Once you have picked an adviser and you get down to recommendations, ask

- Why is it right for me?
- What will I get out of the deal?

- What will the adviser get out of the deal?
- Could I lose money?
- What exactly is guaranteed?
- What are the alternatives?

If any of the following things happen, alarm bells should start ringing:

- A promise of exceptional returns. If it seems too good to be true it probably is.
- Your adviser is vague about the details or cannot explain it clearly without jargon.
- Your adviser says that you must take advantage of a special offer immediately and if you do not sign up now you could lose the deal.
- You are told to cash in some or all of your current investments so that the adviser can reinvest them in something similar. That could mean your adviser simply wants to earn more commission by the reinvestment. This process is known as 'churning' and is illegal unless the original investments really are wrong for you.
- Your adviser recommends that you put all your money into one investment. That breaks the key rule, which is to spread your investments. Recently the FSA suggested that no-one should have more than a third of their investments in one type of stock market investment – and that was reduced to a fifth if it was their only stock market investment.
- Your adviser recommends an investment because of the tax advantages. Saving or avoiding tax should never be the main reason for taking on a particular investment of any kind. Make sure that the investment itself is sound and what you need. Think of investing as a horse; it drives your finances forward. The tax you pay is the cart – the burden that the horse pulls. A light cart will never make a lame horse go fast; so never put the tax cart before the investment horse.

If you do decide to go ahead with an investment, never make a cheque payable to an individual or a firm of financial advisers. Make out your cheque to the firm in which your money is to be invested. If you are being asked to do so, whatever reason is given, walk away.

One of the questions your adviser will always ask is 'what is your attitude to risk?' Most of us, of course, have not got a clue – although if we were asked 'how would you feel if you lost some of your money', most of us would reply 'terrible'. Risk is one thing that advisers are notoriously incapable and ill-equipped to explain. Often they will talk about the 'risk/reward ratio' or some such thing. If you want a reward, they say, you must take a risk. They make it sound like a one-way bet. If you take this strange thing called a 'risk' you will get a bigger reward. In fact, taking a risk means just that – you may get no return on your money, you may lose some of your capital, and you may in extreme cases lose it all. On the other hand you may do well, possibly a lot better than the 4 per cent annual return you can earn in a savings account. Neither is certain: that is why it is a risk. Your adviser may ask you to say if your attitude to risk is high, medium or low, or if you are prepared to take any risk at all. Usually the purpose of these conversations is to get you to agree to put your money into a stock market based investment as that is where the commission is.

Reasons why and key features

After your meeting your adviser will send you a **'reasons why' letter**. This will set out why they are recommending certain products to you. You may be surprised by this letter – sometimes they seem to bear no relation to the conversation you had, especially about risk. Check it carefully, and write to correct it if it is wrong. Many people who have told their adviser they have low to medium desire for risk have ended up with most of their money at risk, whether directly on the stock market or in some cunning variant which seemed a one way bet to wealth, and was – but only for the company that sold it. This letter should also make clear that there is a period in which you can cancel the deal without penalty. It should tell you clearly what this cooling-off period is.

Advisers are also required to advise you of the product's **'key features'**. In other words, they must tell you about its aims, risks and benefits, as well as the impact of charges and expenses. A **personal illustration** must also be given, showing projected costs and fund growth based on the customer's personal circumstances. These documents are very long and can be confusing.

They are also systematically misleading. Part of the document will be an 'illustration' of how the money you have invested might grow. But the rates of growth used in these documents are not promises – they are almost invariably based on standard rates of growth provided by the Financial Services Authority. These rates, which have not changed since 1999, are: 5 per cent, 7 per cent and 9 per cent for tax-free investments such as pensions and some ISAs; and 4 per cent, 6 per cent, and 8 per cent for all other investments which are normally taxed. Often you will see all three growth rates – shown perhaps as low, medium and high. There is absolutely no reason to believe that any of these rates will be achieved. They may be achieved, or not. They may be exceeded or never reached. There is no reason to believe the middle rate will be achieved any more than the low or the high one will.

PROTECT YOURSELF

Understanding the basics of financial products and knowing what you are doing is the best way to protect yourself. Keep up to date by reading the financial sections of newspapers and magazines and listening to programmes such as *Money Box* on Radio 4 and *Working Lunch* on BBC TWO.

The FSA publishes a free booklet, *Guide to Financial Advice*, which gives useful tips on avoiding bad investments. Its website (www.fsa.gov.uk) includes a whole section of consumer advice. You can also read the entertaining guides on the website of www.motleyfool.co.uk which provides a common sense antidote to some of the nonsense the financial services industry would have us believe.

The Financial Services Authority is now one of the most comprehensive and powerful financial regulators in the world. It regulates almost all the investment and savings products on the market, as well as the people who sell them to us and the banks and financial companies that back them. It covers unit trusts, pension schemes, and endowment policies. From 31 October 2004 it will include mortgages and long-term care insurance, and from 14 January 2005 most insurance products will also be covered.

However, some investment and savings products remain outside the scope of the FSA. Current and savings accounts with banks and building societies are covered by a separate Banking Code (which you can find at www.bankingcode.org.uk or from the address on page 235). Also excluded are investments in physical things such as paintings, property, stamps, precious stones, antiques, cars, wine, whisky. Unregulated products such as these are ripe for crooks and scamsters to take advantage of you – as they have over investments in ostriches, wine, champagne, whisky, gold, or property which either did not exist or could not be sold for anything but a large loss. If you come across a scheme like this – avoid it. You can check out the latest rip-off news at www.dti.gov.uk/ccp/scams/page1.htm

Shares, if you buy them directly, including shares in an investment trust (see pages 19–20), are outside the scope of the FSA. However, companies which sell you shares, including advisers and brokers, are regulated and if they give you advice that too will be covered by the FSA. Beware, however, if you buy products directly from newspaper or television adverts or the Internet without seeking any advice. In that case you will probably be on your own – even though they are technically sold to you by a regulated company, the decision to buy is yours and the seller is not responsible for the choices you make.

In general the regulator should make sure that:

■ advertisements for financial products are truthful and not misleading;

■ information about financial products is clear and straightforward;

■ people who sell us financial products are trained and registered; and

■ companies behind financial products are sound and trustworthy.

But everyone still has to be very careful when buying financial products. Firms will still fail, crooks will still try to steal from us, and all investments carry some risk. The regulator cannot protect us against human weakness – greed can still drive both parties to a financial bargain and there will always be fools and knaves in financial institutions as elsewhere. If someone is determined to defraud investors, they will often succeed; and they will often wear a smart suit and drive an expensive car.

One useful service offered by the FSA is its comparative tables of products from different companies. The tables cover investment ISAs, pensions, annuities, endowments and mortgages and more are being added all the time. They allow you to compare charges and costs, although not past investment performance. They are at www.fsa.gov.uk/tables

COMPLAINING

If you believe that you have been treated badly by a financial company there is a simple and clear procedure for complaining. First, you have to decide what exactly you think has gone wrong. Have you been sold the wrong product? Were you misled about it? Has the financial company been negligent, incompetent or dishonest? Even if you bought the product a long time ago, you may still be able to get redress.

When you have decided what has gone wrong, set out your complaint in writing to the Chief Executive of the company concerned. Make sure they know what has gone wrong and what you expect to be done about it. You should get an acknowledgment within a few days and a final answer within eight weeks. If the answer is not satisfactory or you do not get one within eight weeks, your case is said to be 'deadlocked' and you can go to the Financial Ombudsman Service (FOS). The letter from the firm should explain how to do that.

You can complain to the FOS about any firm which is registered with the FSA. That includes banks, building societies, credit unions, investment companies, brokers, Independent Financial Advisers and so on. The complaint can be major – you think you were misled into investing in a risky product – or relatively minor – perhaps your bank has mishandled your instructions over a standing order. The Ombudsman can deal with complaints about any company registered with the FSA even if the complaint concerns a product – such as a current account – which is itself not regulated by the FSA. You have six months from the time your case is 'deadlocked' to go to the Financial Ombudsman.

The Ombudsman will try to resolve the problem quickly by finding a compromise acceptable to both sides. Remember that the principle underlying compensation is that you should be put back in the position you were in before you were mis-sold the product. If a compromise is not possible then the case proceeds to a formal investigation and a preliminary decision by an ombudsman. Normally, the company will accept that. If it does not, it can appeal to the Chief Ombudsman. Once the Chief Ombudsman gives a formal ruling, which can include compensation to the customer, the company has to follow it. There is no direct appeal to the courts, although some companies have tried – unsuccessfully – to get the courts to overturn the Ombudsman's decisions.

The Financial Ombudsman Service is free. You do not need a lawyer to argue your case. If you disagree with the ruling or the compensation ordered then you can still go to court, although that is likely to be stressful, expensive and time-consuming. Further information is available from the FOS.

There are private companies called 'claims handlers' who will offer to take you through the process in return for a hefty slice of any compensation. They are generally not a good idea.

The FOS has faced a huge increase in the number of complaints handled each year and there are delays in dealing with some cases; so you may have to be patient.

You can phone the FOS on 0845 080 1800 or you can find out more from its website (www.financial-ombudsman.org.uk)

COMPENSATION

Sometimes a financial company goes out of business, leaving investors out of pocket, compensation unpaid, or insurance claims unmet. When that happens the Financial Services Compensation Scheme (FSCS) may be able to pay compensation. The maximum amounts of compensation are:

- **Bank or building society account** – you get 100 per cent of the first £2,000 and then 90 per cent of the next £33,000. So the maximum compensation is £31,700.
- If an **insurance** claim is not met because an insurer has gone bust, you get 100 per cent of the first £2,000 and 90 per cent of the rest.
- If an **investment company** goes bust, the maximum compensation is £48,000.

You normally have to ask for compensation within six years of the company going out of business. If your complaint relates to events before 1988, you may find that the FSCS cannot help.

This scheme only applies to firms which are regulated by the FSA. If you invest in a company based in another country (even if the product was sold to you through advertisements that appeared in UK publications or on UK television), you will have to rely on the compensation scheme in that country.

You can phone the Financial Services Compensation Scheme on 020 7892 7300 or look at its website at www.fscs.org.uk

MAKING A WILL

It is not morbid to make a will. None of us lives forever. Making a will not only makes sure that your property is distributed as you want, it also protects your family and friends from difficulties when you die. If you do not leave a will, then your property is divided among your relatives according to strict rules laid down by law. They may not reflect what you want or what your heirs think is fair.

You can do it yourself – every stationery shop has kits to write your own will. But that may be a mistake, albeit one you will never know about. It is much better – and essential in Scotland – to use a solicitor or at least one of the many will-writing companies that you can find on the Internet. Get a few quotes to see what sort of price you are likely to pay; you can reckon on around £60 but it may be more if you need legal advice or have complicated affairs.

Before visiting a solicitor or contacting a will writer, write down all that you own – don't forget your house and car – and decide who you want your things to go to. Remember to consider the implications of Inheritance Tax (see pages 76–83). In Scotland you cannot cut some members of your family out of your will. In England and Wales you can, but dependants can challenge it in the courts. If all the beneficiaries agree, then they can restructure your will after your death.

You will have to name 'executors': people who will assemble your property, sell it if necessary, obtain probate from the courts, pay any Inheritance Tax, and then distribute the proceeds in accordance with your will. Make sure that they agree to the role, and remember that executors may die before you do, so put alternatives in. You can name a bank or a solicitor but they will charge fees.

Your will must be signed by you in the presence of two witnesses who must not be beneficiaries (unlike the executors who usually include beneficiaries). It is only your signature that the witnesses have to confirm, not the contents of the will.

Keep it somewhere safe and tell your family, and especially the executors, where it is. A bank or solicitor will keep it but will also charge you. You can keep it at the local probate registry for £15.

Review your will every few years, as people and circumstances change. It is usually better to write a new will than to sign an amendment (called a 'codicil'). If you marry, any will made before the marriage is invalid, so make a new one. If you do not, then your new spouse will normally inherit all or most of your estate automatically.

Age Concern Factsheet 7 *Making Your Will* is available from the Information Line on 0800 00 99 66.

BOOSTING INCOME

The other side of cutting expenditure is boosting your income. There is money out there you may have forgotten about or did not know you can claim. In your 50s you may have to claim benefits or think a bit about your State Pension – what will it be and can you improve it? Or you may want to strike out before it is too late on a new career or working for yourself.

In this section:

MISSING MONEY

- Tracking money down
- National Savings & Investments
- Unclaimed Assets Register
- National Lottery

SOCIAL SECURITY

- Jobseeker's Allowance
- New Deal 50 Plus
- Tax credits
- Help with the Council Tax

STATE PENSION

- Home Responsibilities Protection
- Married women
- Pension age
- Paying extra contributions
- SERPS and State Second Pension
- Graduated Pension

WORKING FOR YOURSELF

- Career development loan
- Registering as self-employed
- National Insurance
- VAT
- Income Tax
- Avoiding tax

YOUR HOME

- Trading down
- Equity release
- Rent a Room
- Legal rights

MISSING MONEY

If you hit fifty and find that you need extra money, you should check if there is some of your own money lying around that you do not know about. There is an estimated £15 billion of unclaimed assets in bank and building society accounts, National Savings & Investments and insurance policies, as well as unclaimed shares and dividends. Finding this money is much easier than it used to be and can be free.

TRACKING MONEY DOWN

At first sight it may seem strange to think that we might have forgotten about money that is ours. But we are all a bit forgetful, especially about small amounts of cash or shareholdings, and often we may think it is just not worth the trouble of finding. Also people have investments or insurance policies which they tell no-one about. If they die, the information dies with them. We also forget to tell everyone who should be told when we move. National Savings & Investments research found that one in seven of us fails to inform all the financial companies we have dealings with when we change our address. Companies will soon take us off their mailing list when they get letters returned marked 'not known'.

The financial institutions themselves are not as good as they might be at tracking us down – after all they keep the money and have the use of it all the time it remains unclaimed. In Ireland recently the Government passed a law so that assets which had lain dormant for at least 15 years in banks, building societies, the post office and insurance companies were transferred to the State to be used for the public good. Of course, any individual could always claim their own money if they came forward. Within a year of the Act being passed, the banks and building societies had found thousands of people and returned £200 million to them; but that still left another £200 million to go into the fund.

In the UK things are rather more lackadaisical. It is left up to individuals to contact the financial institutions to recover their dormant assets. No-one even admits officially how much there is – although National Savings & Investments says it is £11 billion and the Unclaimed Assets Register estimates £15 billion.

The British Bankers' Association and the Building Societies' Association both have schemes that should help you track down any money that may be languishing with them. Of course, if you know the name of the bank or building society you can go to them. As long as you can establish your right to the money – it was yours or perhaps a relative's – then they will let you have it. If it has been in an account paying interest, the interest will be yours too; but most old accounts pay very poor rates of interest, so it is unlikely to have earned much. Remember, however, that finding an old passbook with money apparently entered in it does not mean that money is still there. Many accounts have been converted from passbooks without the book being finally written up.

If the bank or building society has merged or been taken over, then both organisations will help you track down who owns it now. All old banks and building societies are owned by somebody. There are lists of old names and current owners on the organisations' websites and both have a dedicated Dormant Accounts Scheme that will help you (see addresses on pages 235–236). It does not matter if you don't know whether your money was with a bank or a building society, as the schemes swap information and, although technically separate, they are in practice run as one.

You can check who owns old insurance companies through the Association of British Insurers (see address on page 235), but they cannot look for your policy. Contact the company that currently owns the one where you think you or a relative may have had a policy.

NATIONAL SAVINGS & INVESTMENTS

National Savings & Investments is the only major organisation that does admit how much it has in dormant accounts – £1.5 billion, as well as more than £20 million in unclaimed premium bond prizes. In November 2002 National Savings & Investments launched a free service to try to reunite customers with their money. In the first two years it gave back £7.8 million to more than 10,000 people.

You can get a tracing service brochure from 0845 964 5000 or on the website at www.nsandi.com You can also find out if you have won a premium bond prize directly through the website. You enter your premium bondholder's number – which is not the same as the numbers of your premium bonds – and it searches all unclaimed prizes back to its first draw in 1957.

UNCLAIMED ASSETS REGISTER

One of the problems about finding lost money is that you may have forgotten about it entirely and certainly cannot remember where it is. The Unclaimed Assets Register (UAR) helps to solve the problem of people who may have money with more than 50 financial companies, including major insurers like Prudential and Standard Life, and some of the major companies that were privatised. It is surprising how many people are owed dividends or shares as a result of both the privatisations and the subsequent changes of ownership of the privatised companies.

The UAR does charge a fee of £18, of which it pays £1.80 to charity through a scheme called ShareGift. For that fee UAR searches its entire database for your name and address, including any other names you may have used and all your previous addresses. If it finds any matching data, it will inform you and the financial institution. The rest of the contact is up to you.

The address of the UAR is on page 242. You can do the whole thing online at www.uar.co.uk or call 0870 241 1713.

NATIONAL LOTTERY

Some people forget to claim very large National Lottery prizes. The biggest so far is a jackpot of more than £3 million won in the 6 September 2000 lottery. Sadly it is too late to claim it even if you suddenly think it was you! Lottery winnings have to be claimed within 180 days (about six months) of the draw. After that the money is lost to the winner and goes into the general fund which supports the 'good causes'. So far this fund has benefited from £600 million of unclaimed prizes. You can check if you have an unclaimed prize for any ticket you have bought within the last six months if you have the ticket number.

You can call customer care on 0845 278 8000 or check on the National Lottery website at www.national-lottery.co.uk

SOCIAL SECURITY

In your 50s claiming help from the State can be particularly difficult. The benefit system is aimed at people who cannot work or cannot find work, and it is neither friendly nor generous. Benefits for people under

State Pension age are normally dealt with by the new Jobcentre Plus offices. You can find your nearest one in the phone book or from the website at www.jobcentreplus.gov.uk

JOBSEEKER'S ALLOWANCE

It used to be called Unemployment Benefit and you got it for a year if you had lost your job through no fault of your own and you were available to take a job similar to the one you had done before. After numerous changes, including the significant new name and a cut from 12 months to 6, getting Jobseeker's Allowance (JSA) is much more onerous. Not only do you have to be available for work and actively seeking work, you must also have signed a jobseeker's agreement with the Department for Work and Pensions.

This book cannot go into all the ins and out of Jobseeker's Allowance – even a guide to the rules occupies 100 pages – but some main points are listed below:

- **Available for work** means you must be willing and able to take up a job immediately. Normally that means practically any job of up to 40 hours a week, but if a part-time one comes along then you must be willing to take that. For a short period you can specify that you will only take a job that is similar to, or pays similar money to, the job you have left; that period can be between 1 and 13 weeks and the DWP will decide with you how long it should be.

- **Actively seeking work** means that you have to take steps to find a job; not every day, but certainly several steps during each week. Apart from applying for jobs, 'steps' can include looking at adverts, asking for references, preparing lists of possible jobs, preparing your CV, getting advice.

- **The Jobseeker's Agreement** sets out your availability and the steps you are going to take to find work, as well as things like the kind of job you are looking for and any restrictions you are placing on the work you will do.

All that to get £55.65 a week for six months (a total of less than £1,450). You must also have paid enough National Insurance contributions (although you may be able to get the income-related version if you have not), be capable of work, not be in education, be under State Pension age and live in the UK. If you get a personal or occupational pension of more than £50 a week this will reduce your contribution-based JSA.

One other advantage of getting JSA is that you get a credit to keep your National Insurance contributions going while you get it.

After six months, contribution based Jobseeker's Allowance comes to an end; or rather you can no longer get it on the basis of your National Insurance contributions. Instead, you are subject to a means test to claim what is called income-based Jobseeker's Allowance. You cannot get this if you have savings of more than £8,000 or an income which is above the level of income-based JSA. If you are married or live with someone as part of a heterosexual couple, then your income and savings are considered jointly. So if one of you works, the other cannot claim income-based JSA. Because it is a means-tested benefit, income-based JSA brings your income up to a certain level. That level is £55.65 a week for a single person in 2004–2005 or £87.30 between them for a couple.

Income-based JSA is subject to all the same rules about looking for work as the contribution-based version. It can last as long as you fulfil the conditions.

NEW DEAL 50 PLUS

Once you have been on JSA for six months, you can take advantage of a special programme run by Jobcentre Plus called New Deal 50 Plus. You can also take part if you have been getting Incapacity Benefit or Severe Disablement Allowance for at least six months.

In many ways New Deal 50 Plus is a souped-up version of the ordinary treatment you get at a Jobcentre. You get a New Deal personal adviser who is your contact at the office and they will discuss what you want to do and can do, draw up an action plan to help you get a job, assist with a CV or application letters, look at training opportunities, and even help you find voluntary work which may help you develop skills. Underlying all this help, of course, is the threat that if you do not pursue work vigorously enough then your benefit will be withdrawn.

If you get a job through New Deal 50 Plus you can apply for a grant of up to £1,500 to train to improve your skills, and if you take a low-paid job, then you may qualify for Working Tax Credit (see pages 142–143). People over 50 can get a higher rate of Working Tax Credit in some circumstances.

New Deal also has a special section for people who want to become self-employed. You can get a training grant of up to £1,500 to help you learn the skills you need to run a business and the Jobcentre Plus office will put you in touch with other sources of help for business start-ups. People under 50 on New Deal 25 Plus can get JSA while they are beginning self-employment (but it is not available to people on New Deal 50 Plus).

There is a New Deal helpline on 0845 606 2626 and a website at www.newdeal.gov.uk

TAX CREDITS

Tax credits help two groups of people:

- **Child Tax Credit** is for parents and others who bring up children.
- **Working Tax Credit** is for people in low-paid work, whether they have children or not. People over 50 can get a higher rate than younger people when they return to work after New Deal 50 Plus.

Tax credits can include extra money to help with the costs of childcare, although it is paid as part of Working Tax Credit rather than with Child Tax Credit.

People with children

Child Tax Credit started on 6 April 2003 and most people with a dependent child under 18 can claim it. Child Tax Credit (CTC) replaced the extra amounts for children paid with Basic State Pension and other State benefits. People already getting extra for children with a benefit, however, keep it and can get CTC on top. Child Tax Credit replaced the Children's Tax Credit which had a very short life (two tax years 2001–2002 and 2002–2003).

Despite its name, Child Tax Credit is nothing to do with tax and is paid as a cash amount into a bank account. Unlike the old Children's Tax Credit, it can be paid to non-taxpayers and it can be paid for a child aged 16 to 18 who is in education or looking for work. It comes in two parts:

- **a family element** of £545 a year in 2004–2005 (£10.45 a week) tax free, however many children you have, if your income is below £50,000 a year. The family element is paid at double the rate for the tax year in which a new baby is born; and
- **a child element** of £1,625 a year (£31.22 a week) tax free for each child, if your income is below £13,480 a year.

Child Tax Credit is the same for people in or out of work, and whether they get benefits or pensions or do not. The amount of the CTC does depend on income. If income exceeds £13,480 the annual amount of the child element is reduced by 37p for each £1 above that level. It disappears for one child when your income reaches £17,879 and for two children at £22,279. The family element, however, continues to be paid at those incomes and it does not begin to taper off until your income reaches £50,000 a year. For higher incomes it is reduced by 6.67p for each £1 above £50,000. The minimum family element is £26 and none is paid if your income is more than £57,800 a year.

There can also be extra CTC to help with the costs of childcare for a child up to 15; this can, for example, help parents with two children on an income of up to £43,765 a year. Child Tax Credit is quite separate from Child Benefit. The latter is £16.50 a week in 2004–2005 for the first child and £11.05 for each other child and is paid on top of Child Tax Credit.

People who work

Working Tax Credit (WTC) is paid to people in low-paid work – or who are self-employed with low profits – whether they have children or not. To get it you must normally work for at least 30 hours a week (people who are disabled or who have children only have to work for 16 hours a week). People aged 50 or more who have just returned to work after at least six months on JSA, Income Support or a disability benefit can get extra WTC for a year and need only work for 16 hours a week or more.

Working Tax Credit can be paid at any age. So even if you are over State Pension age and do some work, you may be able to claim it. However, at that age your State Pension – and any other income – will be added to your wages before the calculation is done and may well mean you do not qualify.

Working Tax Credit is higher for couples and lone parents and for people who are more severely disabled. The table below shows the maximum rates of WTC for various categories of people. To get the maximum WTC your income needs to be £5,060 a year or less. However, if you have to work for at least 30 hours a week, then, on the minimum wage of £4.50 an hour, your income will be at least £7,020 a year, so the maximum WTC you can get in practice is just over £28.50 a week. However, if you are aged 50 or more and get the over-50s rate and work between 16 and 21 hours, it is possible to get the maximum WTC, which in that case is £63 a week.

The minimum amount of WTC is 50p a week or £26 a year and the table shows the maximum income you can have and still get some WTC:

WORKING TAX CREDIT 2004–2005
Maximum annual income to qualify

Basic	16–29 hours	£9,241
Basic	30+ hours	£10,977
Disabled	16–29 hours	£14,923
Disabled	30+ hours	£16,659
Aged 50+	16–29 hours	£12,151
Aged 50+	30+ hours	£15,337
Disabled and 50+	16–29 hours	£17,833
Disabled and 50+	30+ hours	£21,020

At these income levels you will get the minimum WTC of 50p a week. To get aged 50 plus benefits you must have been out of work for at least six months before returning to work and be receiving certain benefits.

Income

The calculation of tax credits is based on your income (or joint income for a couple who are married or live as husband and wife). Income includes all pensions, as well as the actual interest earned on your savings or investments. It is not reduced by the total amount of any savings or capital and there is no upper limit to your savings. Income is counted 'gross' before tax or other deductions. The tax credit is calculated on the income in a previous tax year. Once awarded, the amount will not normally change for a year. If your income goes down, you can tell the Inland Revenue and the credit may be increased; but if your income goes up, there is no need to tell the Inland Revenue unless it rises by more than £2,500. You must also inform the Inland Revenue if your personal circumstances change – for example if you move in with someone or you have a child. As the credit is worked out based on income from a previous year, it will be corrected the following year. So do not expect it to be simple or straightforward.

Claiming

Tax credits are claimed from the Inland Revenue. Child Tax Credit is paid into a bank account every week or four weeks. Working Tax Credit is normally paid with your wages. The rules about tax credits are complicated. The application form is 12 pages long and the notes are another 48 pages. You can get a lot more information about it from the Inland Revenue website, and there is a form where you can see how much you will get, although the amount shown is not the annual amount but how much you will get to the end of the tax year. So it can be very confusing. Better is the independent website at www.entitledto.co.uk which will work out your WTC and your CTC and show your entitlement as an annual amount.

The Inland Revenue website (www.inlandrevenue.gov.uk) does allow you to claim online and that can be the easiest and best way to do it. Make sure that you have accurate details of your pay and any other income. Alternatively you can phone 0845 300 3900 (0845 603 2000 in Northern Ireland) or call into a local Inland Revenue Enquiry Centre for advice and to make a claim.

HELP WITH THE COUNCIL TAX

Council Tax is now more than £1,000 a year for the average household. It has risen sharply in the last few years, well ahead of inflation, wage rises and the rise in pensions and other benefits. There are ways to get it reduced which many people are not aware of, however.

If you **live alone**, your Council Tax is reduced by a quarter. You have to apply for this reduction and it can be backdated. If you ask for backdating you may be asked for some proof that you did live alone at that time. If a relationship has ended, a grown-up child has moved out, or a relative has moved on, you should tell the council when that happened. Other sorts of proof may be that the electoral register shows just your name or that your utility bills are in one name not two. Even if someone else lives with you, they may not count – you can still get the reduction as if you lived alone. People who are ignored in the assessment include:

■ anyone under 19 and some recent school or college leavers under 20;

■ students at college or university, including student nurses, youth trainees and apprentices;

■ people who are severely mentally impaired; or

- carers providing care for at least 35 hours a week (except the person's spouse or a child under 18).

If another adult lives with you and has a **low income** of less than £186 a week, then your Council Tax may be cut by 7.5 per cent, 15 per cent or 25 per cent depending on their income.

If someone in the household has a **substantial and permanent disability**, then it is possible that the Council Tax will be moved down one band – which will cut it by around a sixth. If your home is already in the lowest band A, then your tax is cut by one sixth. The property may be placed in a lower band if it has certain features which are important for a disabled person, such as an additional bathroom or kitchen for their use.

Council Tax Benefit

In addition to these concessions your Council Tax may be reduced if your income is very low. A single person in their 50s will get all their Council Tax paid if their income is £55.65 a week or less in 2004–2005. For a couple the figure is £87.30 a week between them. (Some types of income, such as Disability Living Allowance, are ignored when working out your income, while if there are other people living with you the amount of help you get may be reduced.) People with incomes above these levels may get some help. For example, if your Council Tax rate is £1,100, then you will get some reduction if you are single and your weekly income is less than £134 a week – remember you can claim the 25 per cent discount first. A couple will get some help with an income up to £192 a week. Add £25 onto these amounts if you are a carer, or £43 if you are severely disabled. If your Council Tax is less than £1,100 a year, then these weekly amounts to get some help will be lower (of course, they will be higher if your Council Tax is more than £1,100 a year).

Savings over £3,000 will reduce the amount paid and savings over £16,000 mean you get no help at all.

All these reductions apply to homeowners or tenants. Once you reach 60 the rules become much more generous. The lower limits to get all your Council Tax Benefit paid are £105.45 if you are single and £160.95 for a couple. They are higher still at 65 (£121 and £181.20 respectively in 2004–2005). The upper limits to get any help are correspondingly higher too.

To apply for any reduction in your Council Tax contact the local council that sends you your bill (it might be a borough, district, city, or unitary council). In Northern Ireland similar rules apply to your rates – apply through the Rates Collection Agency or the Housing Executive.

Housing Benefit

If you are a tenant you can get your rent reduced, sometimes to zero, on grounds of low income. You apply for Housing Benefit and Council Tax Benefit together, and the rules about assessing income and savings are the same, as are the levels at which you get all your rent paid. Sometimes, however, the amount of benefit you can get is restricted – for example if your rent is considered too high given your circumstances. The upper limits for getting any help at all are different and will depend on your rent.

STATE PENSION

State Pension is on the horizon in our 50s – especially for women who at the moment can draw it at 60, although that will not be true for women now in their early 50s (see page 151). Almost everyone has some entitlement to the State Pension (although for many women only at a very reduced rate) – the good news is that nearly all of us get it, but the bad news is that it does not even pretend to be enough to live on.

Its origins go back to the early part of the 20th Century but the present system is a relic of the 1940s – it reeks of World War II. What you get depends on a complex system of paying contributions at work and 'earning' the right to a pension. Originally the contributions were flat-rate and the pension was a reasonable proportion of the average wage. Today the contributions are seen as just another tax and the pension is barely 16 per cent of average earnings and less than half what you would earn in a week on the National Minimum Wage (which is £4.85 an hour from October 2004). As a result the full pension is well below the poverty line for pensioners. The full Basic Pension is £79.60 a week in 2004–2005 (£4,139.20 a year). Although the pension is very low, a large bureaucracy applies complex rules to decide if you will get it and if so how much.

To get a full Basic Pension you need to have National Insurance contributions for roughly nine tenths of your working life – a period that extends from the age of 16 to 65. At the moment that upper age is 60 for women but those now in their early 50s will have to wait longer (see page 151). So a man needs 44 years $(0.9 \times (65 \text{ minus } 16))$ to get a full Basic Pension. A woman may need slightly less, depending on her date of birth.

Normally these contributions have to be paid with your taxes while you work. However, they can be credited – in other words, you are counted as if you had paid them. There are credits for the years before you are 18 and, for a man, from the age of 60. That rule will extend to women aged 60 or more as their State Pension age rises. You can also get credits for years when you are receiving benefits as unemployed or too ill to work. If you earn at least £79 a week in 2004–2005 but not enough to pay contributions (which starts at £91 a week), then you are counted as if you had paid contributions. Many people in their 50s will have spent some years in education after the age of 18. There are no concessions for this time – if you did not pay contributions then you have a gap in your record.

If you get divorced or are left widowed, and you are not entitled to a full Basic Pension on your own contributions, you can count the contributions of your ex or late spouse instead of your own if that will be better for you. However, you lose that right if you remarry before State Pension age. So if you are widowed or divorced and want to remarry, and do not have a full pension in your own right, it may be worth leaving the wedding until after you reach State Pension age as that way you can benefit from your former or late spouse's National Insurance contributions, which may help you increase the amount of pension you are entitled to.

When you reach State Pension age, your State Pension is worked out by dividing your actual years of contributions by 44 (or slightly less for some women), expressing it as a percentage and rounding it up to the next whole number. So if you are a man who has contributions for 40 years, you will get a pension of 40/44 = 90.9 per cent, which is rounded up to 91 per cent. Currently that would mean a pension of £70.48 a week.

If you have paid contributions for more than the 44 years you need to get a full pension, you do not get any extra – you just get the full pension. If the percentage is less than 25 per cent, then you get nothing.

The State Pension has to be claimed. You should be sent a claim pack a few weeks before you reach State Pension age. If you do not get one, then contact the Pension Service. If you do not claim your pension in time, it can only be backdated for a maximum of three months. It is expected, however, that from April 2005 people will be able to backdate their pension for longer.

HOME RESPONSIBILITIES PROTECTION (HRP)

The sums are done differently for some people who have not worked because they had dependent children or were looking after someone with a disability. Then, each whole tax year spent caring is taken off the qualifying years you need to get a full pension. So a mother who had three children and had not worked for 14 years would need 30 years instead of 44 to get a full pension.

This rule is called Home Responsibilities Protection and to qualify as a parent you must be the one who is paid the Child Benefit. Normally that is the mother and normally it is her career which is interrupted by the children. So you should make sure that the person who takes time off work to care for children is the one who is named as the recipient of the Child Benefit.

Home Responsibilities Protection only applies for tax years from 1978–1979. Before that, if you missed years of contributions because you were bringing up children or caring, they are simply gaps in your record and it is now too late to fill them.

MARRIED WOMEN

To get a full Basic State Pension you must have paid or been credited with full National Insurance contributions. Many married women were encouraged to pay special contributions which earned them no pension at all and were a complete waste of money. None of the years for which they paid these married women's contributions now count towards a pension and you cannot make up the payments for those years to make them count now.

A married women can claim a pension on her husband's contributions. But she has to wait until he has reached 65 (and, of course, has to be over State Pension age herself too). This pension is about 60 per cent of the full pension and in 2004–2005 is £47.65 a week.

If you qualify for a pension on your own contributions and on your husband's, you only get the higher of the two, not both. But you can claim your own entitlement at 60, and then move onto your husband's entitlement when he reaches 65.

PENSION AGE

Since the 1940s women have been able to claim their State Pension at 60 while men have to wait until 65. But for many women in their mid-50s or younger today, that will change. Women born before 6 April 1950 will be able to get their pension at 60. Women born on 6 April 1955 or later will have to wait until they are 65. Women born between these two dates will be able to claim their pension between 60 and 65. Roughly speaking for each month her birth date is after 6 March 1950 she has to add a month to her State Pension age. So, for example, a woman born on 15 April 1951 will have to wait until she is 61 in May 2012 before reaching State Pension age. Someone born on 6 September 1952 will have to wait until she is 62½ on 6 March 2015 to claim her pension.

You can find out your State Pension age from the Pension Service website at www.thepensionservice.gov.uk/resource_centre/calc.asp

PAYING EXTRA CONTRIBUTIONS

It is very easy to miss payments – time spent in education, periods of illness or unemployment where you did not claim benefits, years when you looked after children or other relatives (unless covered by

HRP), time abroad, periods you earned very low pay (less than £79 a week in 2004–2005) will all be gaps in your contribution record. Many married women will have a gap for all the years they worked if they only paid the reduced-rate contributions which earned them nothing.

The result of all these complexities is that more than one in three pensioners gets less than the full State Pension. Most of these – about 3.3 million – are women. But about 350,000 men also currently get a reduced pension.

You can find out what pension you will get by filling in a form to get a State Pension Forecast BR19. You can get the form from the website at www.thepensionservice.co.uk or by calling 0845 3000 168.

Some people in their 50s may find it worthwhile to pay extra contributions to make up their record and give themselves a bigger pension. The Government used to tell people who were paying full National Insurance contributions if they missed a year from paying contributions and invited them to pay the missing amount. But due to a bureaucratic bungle that stopped happening in 1997 and was not restored until 2003. In 2004 the Inland Revenue – which is now responsible for National Insurance contributions – began writing to people about these old gaps and inviting them to pay extra contributions now to fill them. That may or may not be a good idea (see below). You should always ask for a pension forecast before you consider paying extra contributions.

If you have a gap in 1996–1997 or later, then you can pay contributions to cover it as long as you pay them by 5 April 2008. The cost of the contributions will depend when they were due and will be between £309 (for a full year) for 1996–1997 and £361 for the most recent year, 2003–2004. For each extra year you pay, your pension will be raised by either 2 per cent or 3 per cent – the percentage is rounded to the nearest whole number. So that will give you an extra £83 or £124 a year and it will take between 2½ and 4½ years to get back the contributions, or longer if you pay tax. Remember that you can have five missing years without it affecting your State Pension entitlement.

Some people will find they need not bother paying extra contributions. If you are divorced or widowed – and not remarried – you can use the contributions of your husband or wife for any of the years you were married. (See page 221 for more information about the State Pension and divorce.) So you only need consider paying more if you both had a year when contributions were missed. If you are a married woman, then you can get a pension based on your husband's contributions, which is worth about 60 per cent of the full Basic Pension. So it is normally only worth paying extra contributions if they will earn you a pension which is more than 60 per cent of the full pension. It may also be worth paying contributions if you are either older than your husband or less than five years younger. You can get the pension that you have paid for from the age of 60, but you cannot get a pension on his contributions until he reaches 65.

For some of those married women it can be much more worthwhile. If you have paid contributions for less than ten years, then your pension would be less than 25 per cent and pensions that small are not paid. But if paying extra contributions for one or two years will bring you across that threshold, then you go from having no pension to having a pension of around £20 a week. So in exchange for contributions of little more than £300 you may get a pension worth more than £1,000 a year. But remember that you will only get this pension if you do not get one already on your husband's contributions.

Even if you have a gap, and even if filling it would boost your pension – beware. You may be entitled to extra money anyway through Pension Credit. At 60, that will bring your total income up to £105.45 a week if you are single or £160.95 for a couple in 2004–2005. So if you have an income below these amounts, paying extra contributions may not give you any more money.

SERPS AND STATE SECOND PENSION

Since 1978 the Government has provided an earnings-related top-up to the Basic State Pension. It used to be called the State Earnings-Related Pension Scheme (SERPS), but from April 2002 the scheme was altered and is now known as the State Second Pension (S2P). Just to confuse matters even more, both SERPS and S2P when paid are called simply 'Additional Pension'.

This extra pension is paid for through National Insurance contributions. From the start people who belonged to an adequate company pension were automatically 'contracted out' of SERPS. This provided an occupational pension instead of SERPS and both the employee and employer paid lower National Insurance contributions. From July 1988, people who paid into a personal pension were allowed to choose whether to contract out or not and that also now applies to people paying into a stakeholder pension. People paying into a contracted-out occupational pension may be contracted out of SERPS or S2P depending on the type of scheme. In the case of personal and stakeholder pensions, people paying in could choose to carry on paying into SERPS or S2P or could contract out. If they contract out some of their National Insurance contributions are diverted to their pension fund. In addition an extra amount is paid from the National Insurance Fund into their pension fund. This subsidy to encourage people to contract out costs nearly £3 billion a year.

Although many people were advised to contract out of SERPS, many analysts are now changing their minds and advising everyone – certainly everyone in their 50s who is still at work – to pay into S2P as well as their personal or stakeholder pension. That is because the benefits from S2P may be more valuable. They are earnings-related, index-linked and guaranteed by the State. Personal and stakeholder pensions have none of these advantages and as investment performance flags and people live longer, the amount you need to save up to buy a decent pension grows bigger. So to have some of your money in a guaranteed, State-backed scheme makes good sense. Anyone already contracted out of S2P can contract back in – but only from the start of the next tax year. So if you want to do it you should give notice to the Inland Revenue now, so that it will come into effect at the start of the next tax year. People in a good company scheme who are contracted out automatically cannot contract back in; it only applies to people who are in a personal or stakeholder pension.

The new State Second Pension is particularly valuable for lower paid people. As long as you earn at least £79 a week, whatever your earnings, you are treated as if you earned £11,600 a year (2004–2005 rates) and your S2P will be related to that amount, not your actual earnings. Even if your earnings are up to £26,600, you will get more from S2P than you would have got from the old SERPS. People looking after a child under six and some carers and disabled people are also credited in to S2P as though they had earned £11,600 a year.

The result is that nearly everyone who has been employed has an entitlement to a second pension on top of the Basic State Pension. For technical reasons most people who get a State Pension have some small entitlement to SERPS even if they have been contributing to an occupational or personal pension. It is paid from State Pension age and it can be paid even if there is no entitlement to a Basic State Pension. You cannot improve your Additional Pension by paying extra contributions. You can find out your entitlement to Additional Pension by asking for a pension forecast (see page 152).

These rules do not apply to self-employed people. Although self-employed people pay earnings-related contributions, they do not have any entitlement to SERPS or S2P, although that may change in the future.

GRADUATED PENSION

Between 1961 and 1975 everyone in work paid extra National Insurance contributions towards a Graduated Pension. This Graduated Retirement Benefit (to give it its formal name) is not worth much – just a few pounds a week at most and often more like pennies – but it can be the only pension that some married women are entitled to. It is paid on top of any other pension. Even if you think you have no entitlement to a pension, always claim four months before you reach State Pension age to make sure you are getting what you have paid for.

WORKING FOR YOURSELF

Many people see their 50s as a time for a new start, and many things can happen in our 50s that encourage such thoughts. Some of these things are tough – redundancy, loss of a loved one, divorce. Others are mixed – early retirement, inheritance, children leaving home. Others still are just good all round, like an investment maturing and giving you a bit of spare cash, or finally paying off that mortgage and all your debts. Whatever it is, good, bad or indifferent, it may encourage the thought that you should or can do something different: perhaps something you always wanted to do; or maybe you are just fed up with the nine-to-five in the same old job. Whatever the cause, many of us wake up in our 50s and think 'Good grief, is this it?' and we know we just have to do something new.

What better way than to start your own business? It can be as simple as buying and selling things on the Internet through eBay or Amazon; or maybe you are an artist, a musician, a writer; perhaps you can make things, or mend them; or you have the skills from work or life to become what is often grandly called a consultant. Age is not a barrier to these activities. Grey hair, which can be such a disadvantage at work and particularly at trying to get a new job, can give a self-employed person a gravitas that can assist your business.

CAREER DEVELOPMENT LOAN

If you have lost your job or you hanker after a change of direction in your 50s, or you just want to develop skills that you think will be useful for your work in the future, you could consider a career development loan to pay for training.

There is no upper age limit but the course must be vocational – in other words, it must be related to a skill you can use in a job or self-employment – and you must intend to use your qualification to work in the UK or somewhere in the EU.

The course can be full or part time and could be a 'distance learning' course where you do the work mainly at home. You can borrow between £300 and £8,000, although the average is around £4,000, and you can use the money to pay for:

- up to 80 per cent of the course fees;
- other course costs, including a computer or software if you need them; and
- living expenses.

The loan is at a fixed rate of interest and you normally start paying it off a month after you finish the course. However, you can get the repayment deferred for another 17 months if you are out of work, very low paid, or on a government training course. While you are on the course – and while the loan is deferred – the interest is paid by the Department for Education and Skills (DfES). You can repay the loan over a period of up to five years; you can negotiate how long you take with the bank.

Only three banks take part in the scheme. You can choose any of them – you do not have to have an account with them before you apply, although the Co-operative Bank insists you have one when you repay the loan. Comparing the deals on offer is made more difficult by the way the banks calculate the interest they charge. Barclays and Royal Bank of Scotland calculate the interest you pay over the whole period of the loan, including the time taken by the course when you are not repaying anything. Co-operative Bank calculates its interest just over the period when you are repaying the loan. It is better to look at what a loan will cost each month. Here the figures from the banks themselves for a £5,000 loan repaid over three years starting one month after the end of the course:

- **Barclays** £167.79 a month for three years. The bank calls this 7.6 per cent APR calculated over three years of repayments and one year on the course.
- **Co-operative Bank** £170.51. The bank calls this 14 per cent APR calculated just over three years of repayments.
- **Royal Bank of Scotland** £180.55 a month for three years. The bank calls this 10.6 per cent APR calculated over three years of repayments and one year on the course.

When you apply, the bank will assess your credit status and it is possible you will be refused. If that happens you should ask for a reason and check your credit record (see pages 101–102). You can also apply to the other banks in the scheme one at a time.

The DfES has a special website (www.lifelonglearning.co.uk) which brings together information and advice about developing skills and education at all stages of life and includes a section on career development loans. Colleges which offer vocational courses also have information about the loans and there is more information at www.support4learning.org.uk or www.learndirect.co.uk

REGISTERING AS SELF-EMPLOYED

One problem with self-employment is that it creeps up on you. You start by selling the stuff you do not need from your attic, and before you know it you have a regular stall at the local car boot sales; or you are an amateur artist who suddenly finds requests for a local scene in watercolour go beyond friends and family. At what stage, if any, do you become self-employed?

There is no minimum amount of earnings that mean you have become self-employed – what counts more is your intention to make a profit on a regular basis. If you are buying things specifically to sell, if you buy things and sell them within a short time, if you buy and sell regularly, and if you borrow money from the bank to buy them, all these factors argue in favour of your being self-employed. So if you are trading with the intention of supplementing your income and making a profit on a regular and continuing basis, then you are self-employed however little you make. You can get advice from your local Inland Revenue Enquiry Office.

If you start to be self-employed you must register with the Inland Revenue. You have to register separately for both Income Tax and

National Insurance, although you can do them both at the same time. If you want, you can simply write to your local tax office and say that from a certain date you are self-employed. But the safest way is to ring the Inland Revenue's Helpline for the Newly Self-Employed on 08459 15 45 15. They will take your details and register you. Alternatively, booklet P/SE/1 *Thinking of Working for Yourself?* has a form at the back to fill in. It may be a good idea to look at the form before you call the Helpline so that you know the kind of information they will want. With anything to do with the Inland Revenue it is a good idea to keep a copy of everything you send them. Things do get lost.

If you do not register within three months of your first month of self-employment, you will be liable for a £100 penalty. If you have still not registered by 6 October following the end of the tax year when you start up, further penalties may be due. So it is very important to register if you are self-employed.

You can also find out more from the free government booklet *The No-Nonsense Guide to Government Rules and Regulations for Setting Up in Business*. You can get a copy by calling 0845 600 9 006.

NATIONAL INSURANCE

Registering as self-employed automatically obliges you to start paying National Insurance contributions as a self-employed person. You pay two sorts of contributions.

Class 2 contributions are a fixed flat-rate of £2.05 a week (£106.60 a year) in 2004–2005. These contributions count towards entitlement to the Basic State Pension and bereavement benefits for your spouse, as well as Incapacity Benefit if you are too ill to work and Maternity Allowance if you are expecting a baby or a new mother, but they do not give any entitlement to Jobseeker's Allowance if you are unemployed. Everyone who is self-employed has to pay Class 2 contributions unless they apply for what is called 'small earnings exception' (where your profit from self-employment is less than £4,215 in the tax year). You must apply for this exception. There is a form at the back of the leaflet *National Insurance Contributions for Self-employed People with Small Earnings* (CA02). The certificate which gives you this exception can only be backdated for 13 weeks, so it is important to apply for it at the start of the tax year. At that stage, of course, you can only predict your income. If it turns out to be more than £4,215 then you will have to pay the contributions anyway.

If you are self-employed as well as being an employee you must still pay contributions as self-employed. You can apply for exception if your profit is less than £4,215. However, if your profits from self-employment are less than £1,300 a year then you do not need a certificate of exception.

In addition to Class 2 contributions self-employed people also have to pay earnings-related **Class 4 contributions**. These are 8 per cent of profit between £4,745 and £31,720 a year and 1 per cent of profit above that amount. Class 4 contributions are paid with your Income Tax through your annual self-assessment form. Profits for National Insurance purposes are calculated slightly differently from your taxable income – in particular you cannot take off your pension costs before working out your Class 4 National Insurance contributions.

Although these earnings-related contributions can be a significant amount of money – well over £2,000 a year for some people – they give you no extra benefits. In particular, self-employed people are not able to pay into the State Second Pension, although the Government has said it may give them this right some time in the future.

VAT

Self-employed people may have to charge Value Added Tax on their fees or on the goods they sell. Any business, however small, can register for VAT. A business *has* to be registered for VAT if its annual turnover – what it gets in from sales – is more than £58,000.

The VAT system is simple in principle. You charge VAT on your invoices or the goods you sell, which your customers pay to you as part of the price. You also pay VAT to other businesses on goods or services you have bought for your business. Once every three months you add up all the VAT you have charged your customers. You subtract the amount of VAT you have paid to other businesses. You then pay the balance to HM Customs & Excise.

There are two advantages in being registered for VAT:

- it makes you look at every invoice and receipt at least once a quarter; and
- the effect is that you do not pay the VAT on goods and services you buy for your business.

However, there are also disadvantages:

- the paperwork can take a long time;
- if you have customers who are slow payers, you can find yourself paying VAT to Customs & Excise that you have not actually received; and
- if you are busy and fail to pay the VAT by the due date, the penalties can be swift and onerous.

So most people do not register unless they have to. If you do have to pay VAT, two recent schemes make paying it simpler and cheaper for businesses with an annual turnover of £150,000 or less:

The annual accounting scheme allows you to do the detailed calculations once a year. However, you still have to pay your VAT once a quarter on an estimated basis and then send a balancing payment after the end of your year. The scheme does save time each quarter but it removes the discipline of having to do your accounts every three months.

The flat-rate scheme avoids all the complex calculations of adding up the VAT you have charged and subtracting the VAT you have paid and writing a cheque for the difference. Instead, you simply pay each quarter a flat-rate amount of VAT on your whole turnover. The flat-rate amount depends on your business. So, for example, if you are a freelance photographer then you pay 9.5 per cent of your turnover each year as VAT. If you are an accountant you pay 13 per cent. If you run a courier service you pay 5.5 per cent. Remember that these are the percentages of your total turnover including VAT. Once you have paid and deducted this VAT charge, your taxable profit is the rest, so if the scheme saves you VAT, it has the effect of putting up your profit and you pay more Income Tax and National Insurance on that

If you spend more than £2,000 on any one item – perhaps a piece of equipment such as a computer – then you can leave that out of the scheme and deduct the full VAT in the normal way. The flat-rate scheme was made slightly more generous in 2003 and it can be a useful way of saving time and money for a small business. In your first year of registration for VAT the flat-rate percentage is reduced by one percentage point – for example a charge of 10 per cent becomes 9 per cent.

You can find out more about VAT from the Customs & Excise National Advice Service on 0845 010 9000 and from the Customs & Excise website at www.hmce.gov.uk

INCOME TAX

Income from self-employment is added to income from a paid job, a pension, investments and any other source, and you are liable to Income Tax on your total income. You will have self-employed income if you are in business on your own account, even on a part-time or occasional basis, and the money you earn exceeds your business expenses. You will have to fill in a self-assessment form each year and pay your tax on your self-employed income yourself. So it is vital when you start self-employment to set aside a proportion of every penny that comes in to meet your tax bill. A good rule of thumb is to set aside at least a quarter of your gross income (plus the VAT if you are registered) and pay it into a high interest savings account. Knowing you have that sum ready to pay your tax will help you sleep more easily.

Once you have registered as self-employed the Inland Revenue will send you a self-assessment form each April. The form should include the pages for self-employment. If those pages are not included, send for them at once. It will also come with a Tax Return Guide which helps you to fill it in and a Tax Calculation Guide to help you work out the tax that is due. There are also a number of 'helpsheets' which you can either send for or get online at www.inlandrevenue.gov.uk

On this form you declare your business income and expenses. The difference between your gross income and the expenses of the business is your taxable profit. You can think of that as your gross pay if you are an employee. Off that you can take the cost of any pension contributions and any tax allowances you have and then you pay tax on the rest. You also pay Class 4 National Insurance contributions on your profit.

When you start in business it is a good idea to get an accountant. Choose one that is registered with the Institute of Chartered Accountants (see address on page 240).

Business expenses

The self-employment pages expect a breakdown of your expenses in certain categories, such as premises costs, travel and subsistence, interest, repairs. It is worth looking at the categories on the form and arranging your own accounts so that you keep money in the same categories (or at least ones that are easily converted). For example, the Inland Revenue category 'general administrative expenses' can include post, telephone, and office supplies such as paper and pens. If you arrange things in this way, it will save you a lot of time when you come to fill the form in.

There is one category on the form which is simply 'other expenses' – what many people might call 'miscellaneous' in their own accounts. Some things, of course, will genuinely not fall into any other category, but it is best to keep this category as small as possible. It is better to squeeze an expense into one of the Inland Revenue standard categories than have a lot of expenses listed as 'other'. It just makes tax inspectors curious. Get an accountant, at least at the beginning, if your affairs are at all complicated, and keep separate bank accounts.

Sometimes, deciding what is and is not a business expense can be difficult. It is fairly straightforward if, for example, you buy goods and resell them. But other expenses can be less straightforward, particularly when expenses are partly for business purposes and partly private.

Most people begin self-employment by working from home, which means that many domestic expenses become partly business costs.

The most common, of course, is the telephone. Unless you go to the expense of having a separate business line – which can be the best thing to do – your calls will be a mixture of business and personal. The cost of ordering supplies for the business will be a legitimate expense to take off your income, as will a share of the phone rental. But how much? You can work it out by getting an itemised bill, which BT and most other phone companies provide at no cost. Check through one quarter's calls and allocate them to business or domestic. Then work out the proportion of the call charges which are business. Once you have done this exercise, charge that proportion of your total bill to your business. Keep it under review and if you feel that you are spending more time on the phone for business, then adjust the proportion. It is as well to put a note in your accounts to explain that to yourself in the future. You should also keep the evidence for the proportion in case the Revenue ever queries it. Nowadays it is possible to have a phone contract that only charges you for calls, and has no quarterly rental. It might be sensible to get a separate line for business on that basis and then there is no question about what your business calls cost.

You can do a similar calculation for the use of your car. Make a note over a month of how many miles you drive on business and for personal things, and work out the business share. Remember that a drive to the bank to pay in business cheques is a business expense. That proportion can then be used to determine how much you charge of your petrol, your Vehicle Excise Duty, the costs of repairs and servicing, and the cost of buying the car itself.

If you work from home, you can also claim a proportion of the costs of running the house. A share of your gas, electricity, water, and rent if you pay it can all be claimed as a business expense. To work out the proportion, count the main rooms in the house, excluding the kitchen and bathroom. If you work from one room, then count that as a fraction of the main rooms. If, for example, there are two bedrooms, one of which is your office, a living room and a dining room, then there are four main rooms and you mainly work from one of them. So you charge one quarter of the costs of the house to the business.

However, it is important that even the room you use as your business office is used for something else – perhaps it is a spare guest room, or perhaps you use it to listen to music in. If your office is used entirely for the business then this bit of the house may be liable for Capital Gains Tax when you sell your home. So make sure it has an alternative use as well.

It is easy enough when you are first in business to forget to get receipts. Nonetheless, every self-employed person should be an obsessive collector of receipts when they have a business expense. Whenever you buy a newspaper or magazine for your business, take a bus, park the car, or buy a biro, get a receipt and keep It. You will be surprised how they add up. Every pound you spend is 30p off your tax and Class 4 National Insurance, or even more if you are a higher-rate taxpayer.

Capital allowances

Your day-to-day expenses are taken straight off your income and reduce your tax bill for that year. But the costs of larger items that will last for several years are normally not all tax-deductible in the year in which you buy them. Instead, the cost of the equipment is spread over a number of years through a complicated system called 'capital allowances'.

Under this scheme, you can charge 50 per cent of the cost as an expense in the first year and 25 per cent of the balance in the years after that. So if you buy a desk, for example, that costs £250, you can charge £250 × 0.5 = £125 in the first year and then

(£250 minus £125) × 0.25 = £31.25 in the next year and (£125 minus £31.25) × 0.25 = £23.43 in the third year and so on.

The 50 per cent rate does not apply to cars, which are restricted to 25 per cent a year.

Working out capital allowances is quite fiddly, especially as the rules change from time to time. So advice from an accountant or the Inland Revenue can save you money.

Inland Revenue Self-assessment Help Sheet IR222 gives information about business expenses and capital allowances. It can be ordered on the IR Orderline on 08459 000 404 or downloaded from the website at www.inlandrevenue.gov.uk

Keeping records

On the self-assessment tax return you declare your total income and some detail of your expenses and capital allowances. You do not send invoices, receipts, or even accounts. However, you have a legal obligation to keep proper records of your business so that you can work out your income and expenditure and, if it asks to, the Inland Revenue can check your self-assessment form. A small proportion of forms are selected each year for checking, so you may have an investigation at any time. You must keep these business records, including all your invoices, receipts, bank or building society statements, and any other information that may be relevant.

Apart from your legal obligations, every business should have an accounts book which is regularly and accurately written up. If you keep records on your computer, you should always back up the files and print them out regularly. If you have an internet bank or savings account, print out your statements each month and keep them in a file.

If you are self-employed you are legally obliged to keep all records relating to a particular tax year for five years from the date you filed your return for that year. For example, the tax return for 2003–2004 will be due in on 31 January 2005. Five years from then is 31 January 2010. So your records for the tax year 2002–2003 can be destroyed on 1 February 2010. However, if the Inland Revenue has embarked on an enquiry into your tax affairs you have to keep the relevant records until that enquiry is finished.

For more details, see Inland Revenue leaflet SA/BK4 *Self-assessment: A General Guide to Keeping Records*. It can be ordered on the IR Orderline on 08459 000 404 or downloaded from the website at www.inlandrevenue.gov.uk

Accounting year

Although the Income Tax year runs from 6 April to the following 5 April, you can fix any 'accounting year' for your business. That is the year over which you work out your income and expenses and arrive at your profit or loss. Your tax calculation is based on your profit for your accounting year which ends in that tax year. So if your accounting year runs from 1 September to 31 August, then your profit in the tax year 2004–2005 is the profit in your accounting year which ends on 31 August 2004.

When you start in self-employment it can be worthwhile to fix your accounting year to end on 30 April. For example, that would mean the profit from the year 1 May 2003 to 30 April 2004 is taxed in the tax year 2004–2005. If your accounting year runs from 1 April 2003 to 31 March 2004 (just a month earlier), that income would be taxed a whole year earlier in 2003–2004. So by fixing your accounting year to end on 30 April, you in effect put off the tax you pay by almost a year. It also means that you know the exact figures when you come to fill in your tax return.

When a business starts and ends

Special rules apply in the first two years of a new business and when a business ends. For the first year you are taxed on your profit from the date you start until the following 5 April. For the second year you are taxed on your profit for the 12 months up to your accounting date in that tax year, provided that the date is at least a year after your business started. If it is not, you are taxed on your profit for the first 12 months of business.

These rules may mean that some part of your profit is taken into account in calculating your taxable profit for more than one tax year. If so, you are entitled to 'overlap relief' when your business ends, the effect being that, over the lifetime of your business, you are taxed on no more and no less than the full amount of your profit. All this gets very complex and it is worth consulting an accountant, at least in the first and last years of your business.

The self-assessment timetable

The self-assessment timetable is peculiar and full of penalties. If you are subject to self-assessment in 2003–2004 you should have been sent a tax return in April 2004. This form relates to your income and allowances for 2003–2004. The form can be returned at once and absolutely has to be returned by 31 January 2005. If you miss that deadline, there is an automatic £100 penalty. However, if the tax you owe is less than £100 then the penalty is reduced to equal the tax you owe. If you owe nothing the penalty is zero. If you do owe tax and that is not paid by 31 January, then interest is charged. There is more detail on the timetable and penalties below.

Income Tax is charged on income received in the current tax year. The tax is due on 31 January and 31 July, with any balance due the following 31 January. The tax year runs from 6 April to 5 April, so before the end of the tax year, on 31 January 2005, you are expected to pay half the tax due on income which has come in from 6 April 2004 to 5 April 2005. That is clearly impossible to do accurately as you cannot know how much your income will be from 1 February to 5 April. So the tax you pay is an estimate and the payments you make are 'on account'; in other words, they will be revised in the following year from the information in your next tax return.

This is the timetable:

- **April 2004** – tax returns are sent out for the tax year 2003–2004. The taxpayer completes with the details of income and allowances for 2003–2004. That information is used to calculate exactly the tax that was due in 2003–2004. You may have already made payments of this tax in January and July 2003.
- **30 September 2004** – if the form is sent back by this date, the Inland Revenue will calculate the tax due in 2003–2004 and the estimated amount of the tax due in 2004–2005 in time for the 31 January 2005 payment. Even if your return is in later than 30 September, the Revenue will still calculate the tax but may not do so in time for the 31 January 2005 deadline. In that case, the taxpayer has to work this out themselves.
- **31 January 2005** – half the estimated tax for 2004–2005 is due. This is an estimate (called a 'payment on account'). Any overpayment or underpayment for 2003–2004 is corrected. If there was an underpayment, a further payment is due. If there has been an overpayment, then a refund is due. Normally, the extra money or the refund is simply added on or taken off the tax due on account for 2004–2005.

If your income goes down significantly from one year to the next, then your estimated tax – which is based on the previous year's income – is likely to be more than the amount actually due. In that case you can tell the Revenue and pay less on account. However, if it turns out you got it wrong and you pay too little tax, you will be charged interest on the unpaid tax back to the date it was due.

If the balancing payment for 2003–2004 is less than £2,000, and you have earnings or possibly a pension that is taxed through PAYE, this tax can be collected through PAYE but only if you get your tax return back by 30 September 2004.

The key dates and penalties for tax returns for 2003–2004 (sent out in April 2004) are:

- **April 2004** – tax returns for 2003–2004 are sent out to 9.5 million people.
- **30 September 2004** – if your form is received by this date, the Inland Revenue will calculate your tax by the time it is due. If you miss this deadline, then the Revenue may still get the calculation done in time. If your form misses this date, you will not be able to arrange to pay extra tax due through the PAYE system.
- **31 January 2005** – you must send back your tax return by this date. The penalty for missing this date is normally £100 (but if you owe less tax than £100 the penalty cannot be more than the tax due). If you do not owe any tax you will not have to pay the penalty. The Revenue will not impose the penalty if there is what it calls a 'reasonable excuse' for the form being late. That really only means serious illness or bereavement; pressure of work, or not noticing the various letters from the Inland Revenue will not be accepted. There may also be a daily fine of £60 for each day the form is late, although this penalty is not automatic and can only be made after a judicial process.

■ **31 January 2005** – the balancing payment for 2003–2004 is due and so is the payment on account for the tax year 2004–2005. Penalty interest is charged on unpaid tax for every day it is late. At the start of 2004 this rate was 6.5 per cent a year.

■ **28 February 2005** – a 5 per cent surcharge is added onto any tax due for 2003–2004 which is still not paid.

■ **28 March 2005** – interest is now charged on the surcharge if that has not been paid.

■ **31 July 2005** – if the tax return has still not been submitted, a second £100 penalty is imposed.

■ **31 July 2005** – a further 5 per cent surcharge is added to any tax due for 2003–2004 which is still not paid.

■ **28 August 2005** – interest now begins to be charged on the second penalty if that has not been paid.

Everyone who is sent a tax return has a 'tax account' opened at the Inland Revenue. You will receive a Statement of Account once a year showing the money you owe, and also in certain other circumstances, including:

■ when there are changes to items in your account;

■ when a tax payment is due in the next 35 days;

■ every two months when between £32 and £500 is due;

■ every month when over £500 is due;

■ when the Inland Revenue has arranged for unpaid tax to be collected through PAYE; or

■ when you have paid more tax than is due.

You should check your Statement of Account when you receive it and contact the Inland Revenue if you disagree with the entries. A small number of tax returns are selected for investigation; they are called 'enquiries'. Usually this is because something appears wrong, or if the figures have changed significantly from one year to the next, but some tax returns are selected at random. If your figures do change from one year to the next – for example, a sudden large capital allowance or a category of expenditure suddenly grows – you can add a note on the form explaining why.

If you have asked the Inland Revenue to calculate your tax bill, or you have calculated your tax but the Inland Revenue has changed your figures, you will be sent a Tax Calculation. You should check that the figures are correct and that you agree with any changes made. If you want to amend anything you should let the Inland Revenue know as quickly as possible. The Revenue admits that it gets around half a million self-assessment calculations wrong. So checking them is always worthwhile.

The Inland Revenue has a Self-Assessment Helpline on 0845 9000 444 which can provide help or send out leaflets.

AVOIDING TAX

People who are self-employed often seem to resent paying tax more than employees do. It is probably because they have the money upfront and then have to give large amounts of it to the Inland Revenue, whereas an employee is simply given their money net of tax and, although they may complain, they never have to turn over any of 'their' money to the taxman. Just to rub salt in the wound, self-employed people also have to do the all the hard work of assessing how much tax they owe! The other reason is that National Insurance can be very onerous and yet pays for so little – principally a flat-rate State Pension worth barely £4,000 a year.

One popular way to try to reduce the tax bill has been to 'incorporate'. The principle is simple. Instead of being a self-employed individual (a 'sole trader' in the jargon), you form a company of which you are the sole director. The company then does all the business. As director you make your money in two ways: first, you pay yourself £4,745 a year; second, as director you take the profits of the company as a dividend rather than as pay.

The first tax saving is that there is no National Insurance charged on dividends. However, although you do not pay National Insurance contributions, your earnings are above £79 a week which ensures that you are credited with a contribution to protect your State Pension. There is no tax on your earnings as you are paid exactly at the threshold for tax becoming due. This amount is deducted from the company's profits. As it is a small company it pays tax at 19 per cent on profits up to £50,000. The after-tax profits are then distributed to you as a dividend on which you pay no basic-rate tax and, If you pay higher-rate tax, then that is paid at just 32.5 per cent. These rules were tightened in the 2004 Budget. Nonetheless, a sole trader with a turnover of £15,000 could save £1,000 a year in tax and National Insurance by incorporating; someone making £50,000 could save £4,000.

Tackling incorporation is not the first time the Government has acted to prevent tax avoidance through working for yourself. In March 1999 it slipped an innocuous press release into the Budget papers. It was called IR35 *Countering Avoidance in the Provision of Personal Services*. It said 'There has for some time been general concern about the hiring of individuals through their own service companies so that they can exploit the fiscal advantages offered by a corporate structure'. The concern was that people were leaving companies as employees and then immediately hiring themselves back as contractors. It was common in the 1980s and seemed to help everyone – the companies reduced their employee headcount, cut their obligation to pay National Insurance and pension contributions, and avoided both the expense of holiday and sickness pay and the inconvenience of employment tribunals if they wanted to get rid of someone. The individual gained a certain freedom, was probably paid more, and ended up paying less tax and National Insurance – the move was often combined with setting up their own 'service company' or partnership.

IR35 was to change all that. In future, anyone hiring their labour back to a company through their own service company was to be subject to strict new tests. In effect these looked at whether their work still had the characteristics of employment – in other words, did they still have a 'boss' at the company they reported to, could the company decide what, when, where, and how the work was done, could the contractor use another person instead to do the work or was the work specific to him or her, did the contractor provide their own equipment and work on the company premises, were they paid a fixed and pre-agreed sum for the job or was their pay on an hourly basis, were there any conditions in the contract which looked like employment (sick pay, holiday pay, rights on termination of the contract and so on).

If the Inland Revenue determines that the work is 'like' employment, then the contractor has to pay tax and National Insurance on any money received from fees from that customer. It was once described as being fair only in the sense that it combined all the disadvantages of being an employee with all the disadvantages of being self-employed. The rules were challenged in the courts but in December 2001 the Court of Appeal ruled in favour of the Inland Revenue and refused leave to appeal to the House of Lords.

The effect is that people who contract their services to companies and work on the company's premises will usually be subject to the rules now universally known as IR35. To avoid them you have to have many clients, provide your own equipment, set your own hours, and be able to make a loss on the contract. So in other words you have to be genuinely self-employed; otherwise IR35 will bite. The people mainly affected are in the IT business, but it can affect anyone.

Following the introduction of IR35 the Professional Contractors Group was formed to protect the rights of freelancers. You can download a free guide to freelancing from its website is at http://www.pcg.org.uk There is official information on IR35 at http://www.inlandrevenue.gov.uk/ir35

Beware of schemes that pay you to work at home but where you have little choice about what you do. These can really be employment, not self-employment. You can get guidance on how these are defined from the Inland Revenue leaflet IR56 *Employed or Self-employed?*

YOUR HOME

Many people in their 50o livo in a house worth a pools win but find they have too little money to live on. Converting the booming value of property into an income is one of the great challenges of the age. People in their 80s, or even 70s, can convert their home to a regular income relatively easily. But in your 50s you are just too young. There is more about traditional 'equity release' products later – they are called that because you set free some of the value or 'equity' – in your property. First, however, why not just move?

TRADING DOWN

The simple way to make money from your house is to sell it and buy a cheaper one. It may sound radical and dramatic but it is the best way to release value from your home. It is not without cost – estate agents, lawyers, surveyors and, of course, removal contractors will all want to be paid. They know that moving is a time when large amounts of money pass through our hands, and also one of great anxiety, so they usually take the opportunity to charge a lot. There will also usually be Stamp Duty Land Tax to pay on the new property. Despite all these costs, however, it is the cheapest and best way to release value from your home.

What it will cost

Solicitors will charge you at least £350 for the conveyancing itself. Often it will be more, especially if the new home is expensive. If you are buying and selling you can double that. In addition there are searches to be done to make sure the home you are buying will be legally and safely yours. Altogether you can easily reckon on £1,500 plus VAT for lawyer's fees. Of course, all these costs are higher in London and the south east of England.

Estate agents act for the seller. So if you are buying they are not on your side, however pleasant they may seem. When you sell they will charge you between 1 and 2 per cent of the price paid for your home. So with the average house now costing £140,000, estate agents charge between £1,400 and £2,800 plus VAT for the average sale. In London, where prices are higher, the percentage may be even more. It is always worth negotiating and looking for lower cost agents in your area. Always make sure too that the fee is inclusive – you do not want to find that you have to pay for photographs or advertising on top.

If you are buying on a mortgage then the lender will demand a survey, but that is just for a valuation to make sure that the loan is a good risk. Although you pay, this survey will tell you nothing that you want to know. For a real survey you have to pay more. It can cost around £500 but it is worth it. Apart from anything else it may help you haggle down the price – and save you more than it costs.

The removal company will also want paying. The cost depends on how much stuff you have, what service you want, and how far you are moving – but reckon on £500 to £1,000. If you have to store your things to cover the gap between buying and selling, then reckon on £100 a fortnight.

Stamp Duty Land Tax

Stamp Duty Land Tax (SDLT) is the new name for the old Stamp Duty and it applies whenever you buy a home.

SDLT rates

Price of property	Rate of tax
Up to £60,000	Nil
£60,001–£250,000	1 per cent of total price
£250,001–£500,000	3 per cent of total price
£500,001 and above	4 per cent of total price

SDLT is a strange tax. Once you cross a threshold it is calculated at that rate on the whole price. So if you buy a home for £250,000 the SDLT is 1 per cent or £2,500. But if the house costs £250,001 then SDLT is 3 per cent, which is £7,505. In other words, £1 on the price puts an extra £5,005 on the tax! The odd fiver comes about because SDLT is always rounded up to the next £5.

There are two ways to keep down the cost of SDLT:

Disadvantaged areas – in some parts of the country the nil rate of SDLT applies up to £150,000 instead of £60,000. You can check if the property you are buying is in one of these disadvantaged areas by entering its postcode on the Inland Revenue website at www.inlandrevenue.gov.uk/so If your property *is* in one of these areas – and many of them are very attractive despite the label – you can save up to £900.

179

Pay for some things separately – the other way to cut the tax is to negotiate with the owner to buy things such as carpets, curtains, and other movable fittings separately – no tax is due on what you pay for them. This tip can be particularly useful if the cost of the property you are buying is just above one of the thresholds and you can bring the price down below the threshold and cut the tax from 4 per cent to 3, or, even better, from 3 per cent to 1. But even if you do not cross a threshold, by paying £2,000 for the carpets, curtains and the large table left in the dining room, you can save £60 on the tax on a house in the middle band. Generally, you can pay separately for items that can be moved and these include carpets, curtains and blinds, freestanding furniture, kitchen white goods, electric and gas fires that are removable, and light shades and fittings. Other items such as fitted kitchen units, built-in Agas and wall-mounted ovens, fitted bathroom units and sanitary ware, central heating and intruder alarms count as part of the house and cannot be separated from the purchase price. There is guidance on the Inland Revenue website. You should also make sure that you do not pay more than these items are worth. The Inland Revenue is on to that trick and may well investigate deals around the thresholds. The buyer is responsible for assessing the amount of SDLT and paying it.

Cost of moving home

	Old home	New home		Profit
	£250,000	£150,000		£100,000
			Total	
Solicitor	£500	£1,000	£1,500	
Estate agent	£3,750		£3,750	
Survey		£500	£500	
SDLT		£1,500	£1,500	
Moving		£750	£750	
			£8,000	£8,000
			Net profit	£92,000

So selling a home worth £250,000 and buying one worth £150,000 could easily cost you £8,000, leaving you with a net profit of around £92,000 to use for your future. Although spending £8,000 may seem a lot, it is still the cheapest way to release value from your home. You can cut all these costs too if you are prepared to do more work yourself – from advertising it in the paper to hiring a van for the move. You can even do the conveyancing if you want (the Consumers' Association produces a guide on how to do that).

EQUITY RELEASE

If you do not want to move home then there are other ways to raise money from your home. One way you should *not* consider is the standard equity release product. These are only suitable for people of 70 or more, although some companies will sell them to people in their 50s. There are two main sorts of equity release products currently on the market:

Roll-up loans

A roll-up loan is simply a mortgage on your home but you do not make any monthly payments. Instead, the interest on the loan is added to your debt each year – in other words, it 'rolls up'. So each year your debt grows. When you finally die, your home is sold and the debt is repaid. The only schemes worth considering are those that guarantee your debt can never exceed the value of your property and that you are safe to stay there all your life, if you want. Nowadays these products are called 'lifetime mortgages'. The interest charged on a roll-up loan is at least 7 per cent, which is very high when you consider that you can get a regular mortgage at a shade over 5 per cent fixed for 25 years. The companies say that is because it can be many years before the debt or the interest will be paid.

Such a high mortgage rate means that by the time you die the whole value of your home can have disappeared. For example, someone aged 70 with a house worth £160,000 can borrow around quarter of that amount (£40,000). If they live 20 years, then at 7 per cent that debt will have grown to £160,000, which is as much as your home is now worth. Of course, the value of your home may also have grown, but you cannot guarantee that. So it is possible that having £40,000 now will cost you the entire value of your property. It also means you cannot know how much of the value of your home will be left for your children – it may be safest to assume it will be nothing.

You may find a company that will do a roll-up loan for someone as young as 55. But at that age you will only be able to borrow at most about 10 to12 per cent of the value of your home. You should avoid them until you are at least 65 if you can. Even at that age you can only borrow about 20 per cent of the value of your home. At 75 that rises to around 35 per cent and at 85 it is about 45 per cent. So hang on.

Home reversion schemes

A home reversion scheme is rather different. You sell a share of your home to a finance company for a cash sum. You will always get a guarantee that you can live there for as long as you want. You do not borrow any money, so there is no debt ticking up. But the finance company owns a proportion of your home and as the value of your home rises, so does the value of the company's share. You do at least know what proportion will be yours to leave to your heirs, and if you need more money in a few years you can sell another portion of it.

However, home reversion schemes cannot normally be found for anyone under 65 and even then there are restrictions on the value of your home. How much you will get will depend on your age and sex – women live longer, so get less at a given age than men, and couples get least of all because the company does not get its money until both partners have died or gone permanently into residential care. For example, a single man aged 70 with a £200,000 home who took a home reversion scheme on half of it might get a lump sum of around £48,000; a single woman would get £44,000 and a couple just £40,000. But in your 50s, forget it.

Points to consider

If you do consider a scheme to raise money on your home, consider carefully what you want the money for. These schemes are long-term financial deals, so make sure the advantage you get is long term too. It is not sensible to mortgage part of your home for life to go on a holiday or pay off a credit card debt. It may be sensible to use it to pay for a major home repair or improvement that will enhance the quality of your life. However, if you need repairs it is better to take out a straightforward second mortgage if you can afford the monthly repayments. Alternatively the Home Improvement Trust (see address on page 239) is a charity that helps people who want to release equity specifically to pay for home repairs and may offer a better deal than a commercial lender.

If you do borrow money from the value of your home, then you can convert it into a income for life. You can do that by buying what is called a purchased life annuity. But, again, in your 50s your age is against you. At 55 a man can expect around 24 years of life and a woman 27 years. People who take out annuities will probably beat those ages by five years. So any company that promises you an income for life has to reckon on a very long payment time.

So if you raised even £100,000 from your home one way or another, a single woman aged 55 would get an income around £421 a month for life. A man would get £470. A couple would get rather less, depending on their ages. Non-taxpayers would get slightly more. Younger people would get less, and older ones would get more. (There is more about purchased life annuities on page 24.)

You should also be aware that if you claim, or will claim in the future, any means-tested benefit such as Income Support, income-based Jobseeker's Allowance, Pension Credit, Housing Benefit, Council Tax Benefit, or Child or Working Tax Credit, then any extra income could reduce those benefits – possibly to zero.

From 31 October 2004 mortgages – including roll-up loans – and the companies and individuals who sell them will be regulated by the Financial Services Authority. That means there are clear complaints procedures if you are not happy with the scheme you have been sold. The Government has announced that home reversion schemes will also be regulated by the FSA – as legislation will be needed, this may not happen until 2005 or 2006, however.

Always make sure that you understand the scheme you buy and are happy with it. Get independent advice. If you have children or others who may expect to inherit your home, tell them what you are doing.

The Age Concern publication *Using Your Home as Capital* gives detailed information about equity release schemes (see page 247).

RENT A ROOM

If you do not want to move and you decide against borrowing, one obvious way to make money from your home is to take in a lodger. Under the Inland Revenue Rent a Room scheme, rent from a lodger is completely free of tax as long as it does not exceed £4,250 in the tax year (that is rent of around £81.50 a week or £354 a month). To qualify the person has to be a lodger rather than a tenant – they must share some rooms with you (kitchen or bathroom or living rooms) and maybe eat with you from time to time.

You can have more than one lodger under the scheme, as long as the total rent from all your lodgers does not exceed £4,250. If the rent does go over £4,250 then you can either pay tax on the excess over that amount or you can work out your profit from the whole deal and pay tax on that. You can choose whichever method is better for you. Once you have gone over the limit you may want to consider letting out more of your home. You can offset against the rent all the costs of the letting, including a share of the costs of gas and electricity, water charges, insurance, maintenance and repairs, Council Tax and any costs associated with finding or managing the lodgers. If you have a mortgage you can charge a share of that too.

Even if you stick within the tax-free £4,250 limit, you may have to pay Capital Gains Tax if you sell your home and it has increased in value while you had the lodgers. In practice if you have just let one room under the Rent a Room scheme it is unlikely that you will have to pay Capital Gains Tax. If you did let out a substantial part of your home, however, then Capital Gains Tax may have to be paid. (See pages 73–74 for more details on Capital Gains Tax.)

If you let the room to a member of your family, you can still claim the Rent a Room allowance as long as it is a genuine financial arrangement. No Capital Gains Tax charge can arise on the part of the property you let to a family member.

LEGAL RIGHTS

If you live in the same property as your lodger, then you are classed as a resident landlord and there should be no problems about getting rid of a lodger you do not want to remain. However, it is probably as well that you make it clear they are not a tenant. Even though they will have their own room, you will retain the right to enter it and, for example, to clean it or change the bed. The lodger is there under licence, not as a tenant. Normally, they have the right to remain there just for the period that the rent is paid. So if the rent is paid monthly in advance, they will be able to stay until the end of the month. However, if the person has exclusive rights to the room and you cannot enter without permission, then they will be a tenant and that gives them stronger legal rights and may cause you more problems if you want to get rid of them or you want to sell your home. A tenancy agreement has to be honoured by a new owner, but a licence does not.

If you let several rooms to several people, then you can be counted as a House in Multiple Occupation and that imposes severe obligations on you to provide such things as fire escapes and proper sanitation. It is best avoided. Nevertheless, even if you let one room to a lodger, you are obliged to make sure that any gas appliances they use conform to safety rules and that you have an annual safety check by a registered person. Electrical items that you supply must also be safe to use, as must any electrical supply used by the lodger. You do not normally have to follow the rules that apply to professional landlords for the fire safety of furniture, although obviously it is sensible if all your own furniture conforms to the rules and any furniture purchased since 1988 should do so. Furniture made before 1950 is exempt from the regulations.

You can find out more in *Landlords: A Guide to Landlords' Duties – Gas Safety (Installation and Use) Regulations 1998* from the Health and Safety Executive (www.hse.gov.uk).

If you have a mortgage, you will normally have to get permission from your lender to let out any rooms. If you are a tenant yourself, then you will have to tell your landlord. Many tenants will also have to get permission, although secure council tenants do not need permission to take in a lodger. You should also tell the company that insures your home and its contents. You may have to pay more; and it is unlikely that the lodger's belongings will be covered by your contents insurance.

If you lived alone before letting the room, then the 25 per cent discount on your Council Tax will normally stop from the time the lodger moves in. However, if the lodger is in a category which is exempt from Council Tax, such as a student, then the discount will continue (see pages 145–146). Any income you get from a lodger will normally affect your entitlement to means-tested benefits or tax credits.

For more information see Inland Revenue leaflet IR87 *Letting and Your Home*. Copies are available from tax offices, the IR Orderline on 08459 000 404 or the website at www.inlandrevenue.gov.uk A useful booklet from the Office of the Deputy Prime Minister called *Letting Rooms in Your Home: A Guide for Resident Landlords* sets out a lot of the legal matters and the other things you should check – ask your local Citizens Advice Bureau for a copy, or download one from www.odpm.gov.uk

---

LIFE CHANGES

Death is not something most people happily talk about. But once you reach your 50s you know one thing is almost certain – you are more than halfway through your life. Very few people live to 100 and almost none until they are 120. So your 50s are more than halfway. In fact halfway is reached while a man is 38 and a woman is 40. It is not morbid to think of these things; it is very practical. Having some idea of how much time is left does help us plan – how long we want to work, how long our retirement will be, and how long our savings have to last. It also lets us look at what we might want to do with our remaining time and think about some of the things we may have to deal with.

In this section:

LONGEVITY

RIGHTS AT WORK

- Protection against dismissal
- Redundancy
- Ageism
- Other discrimination
- Working on
- Flexible retirement

DISABILITY

- Discrimination
- Disability benefits
- From career to carer

RELATIONSHIP BREAKDOWN

- Divorce
- Separation
- Same sex couples
- Unmarried couples

MOVING ABROAD

- Making the decision
- State benefits
- National Insurance
- Occupational or personal pension
- Tax
- Buying property
- Motoring
- Health

LONGEVITY

People in their 50s today can look forward to a longer life than any previous generation of humans could, and life goes on getting longer.

The life insurance industry began in the 18th Century when researchers began to consider for the first time that mathematics could be applied to the length of the human life. At first it was fairly crude – researchers went round graveyards writing down the ages at which people died. Mathematical techniques were developed to use this information to make predictions about how long people would live and what was a reasonable price to charge for life insurance or for a pension for life (an annuity).

Nowadays the life insurance industry uses what it calls 'Life Tables' produced from its own evidence of the length of time that people live who have life insurance products. It is important for them to have this information, as they have to know how much they can pay out for life and still make money. Annuitants tend to live longer than other people: not because they have a stake in surviving but because they tend to be wealthier and better educated and both those things lead to longer life.

The Government Actuary's Department (GAD) also produces tables of life expectancy. The figures used here are for the whole of the UK and are for the years 2000 to 2002. They show the age at which half the population will have died. So if you are a 55-year-old woman you can expect to live about 27½ years (until you are 82½). In other words, if you take the whole population of 55-year-old women in the UK, half will die before they reach 82½ and half will die after that age. Women tend to live longer than men, so the tables are separated by sex. They show that women in their 50s can on the whole expect to live to until they are around 82 or 83. Men in their 50s can expect to live around four years less, to around 78 to 79.

Over the last 20 years these figures have both grown – by around 3½ to 4 years for men in their 50s and around 2½ to 3 years for women. The latest figures show that they will grow faster in future. The GAD says that by 2031 life expectancy at birth will rise by a shade over 5 years for men and a shade under 4½ years for women. These figures are around 1½ years more than was assumed as recently as 2001.

Of course these crude averages hide many differences – for example, smokers will die sooner, and people in Scotland die younger than people in other parts of the UK. The healthier and the wealthier you are, the longer you can expect to live. But the tables give you some idea of what your life expectancy might be – and that may help you plan for those years.

RIGHTS AT WORK

At the moment there is no legal protection against discrimination on grounds of age. That will change from December 2006 (see pages 197–199). But until then everyone in their 50s has to be aware that they may not be called for a job interview, may be overlooked at work for promotion or training, or may be selected for redundancy on grounds of age alone – and there is little that can be done about it.

PROTECTION AGAINST DISMISSAL

Every employee does have protection against unfair dismissal once they have been with an employer for at least a year. Before that you can be sacked without a reason, although any decent employer will give you one. After that there has to be one of a very limited number of reasons for dismissal (normally related to your ability or qualifications to do the job or your conduct). Redundancy is another valid reason but there are rules about how people are selected for redundancy (see below). You cannot be dismissed because of trade union membership or activity or if you raise a health and safety issue. Women cannot be dismissed on grounds of pregnancy and men are now protected from dismissal for taking statutory paternity leave. Even if you have not been dismissed but your working life has been made so difficult that you have felt you had to leave, then you may have a case for what is called 'constructive dismissal'; in other words, you have effectively been prevented from doing your job.

You can get help with dismissal or work problems from a trade union, a Citizens Advice Bureau, local law centre or advice agency or from a lawyer specialising in employment law. You can get initial advice free by email from many specialist lawyers now. You can find lists of lawyers and sources of advice on employment law at www.venables.co.uk Alternatively you can try the website of the Law Society for England and Wales at www.lawsociety.org.uk or www.solicitors-online.com (or in Scotland at www.lawscot.org.uk), which allow online searches for solicitors by both area and speciality.

REDUNDANCY

Redundancy used to be the great destroyer of jobs for people in their 50s. When it comes to compulsory redundancy, the rule is often 'last in, first out' – in other words, new members of staff are chosen first. But when it comes to voluntary redundancy it is often quite the opposite. Although less common a practice than it used to be, older employees are sometimes targeted and bribed with promises of pension protection, large redundancy payments and sessions with redundancy counsellors. Employers know that people are attracted by the idea of being able to take away a large lump sum and a pension, and that they don't necessarily think through how they will live in five years' time. If a voluntary early retirement package, on reasonable terms, is offered, people queue up for it and the union is often pushed aside.

Employers may prefer to make older employees redundant because it frees up the promotion ladder for younger people, which is supposed to boost morale lower down; and managers want new blood and assume that people who have been doing a job for some years are stale. Both these reasons are ageist – they discriminate solely on grounds of age – and many companies which have followed them to get rid of many people over 45 realise too late that they have lost a valuable resource. It has been called the collective memory of the company.

There is also a very practical reason why companies try to bias redundancy towards older workers. Many salary structures give increments for service. So if there are two people doing the same job, the one with longer service with the company will be paid more, sometimes a lot more, than the other. So getting rid of long-serving staff, who by their nature will tend to be older, saves more money, both on salary and pension contributions, than making newer employees redundant. That is why enhanced terms are often offered – it costs the company money this year but saves it money in future years.

Sometimes these deals will be offered with very little time to decide. Treat that like any offer you are pressured into taking – ask for more time and do not accept it if that is refused.

Redundancy is one of the valid reasons for dismissing someone. It means that the company no longer needs that job to be filled – whether through technological advance, a decision to do without that post, or a decline in business activity. It is the post not the person which is made redundant. So once the employee has gone the business cannot just fill it again. Redundancy is a dismissal. So if you volunteer for redundancy it is important to make sure that your employer does actually dismiss you. It is always wise to make sure that you get a letter from your employer setting out the terms of your dismissal and confirming that it is due to redundancy. Without that you may find problems with either the Inland Revenue or and the Department for Work and Pensions when you come to claim benefits.

If you are made redundant it is very important that the employer has made the selection for redundancy fairly. If you do not want to be made redundant and you suspect that you have been chosen because of trade union membership or lawful activity, parental responsibilities or leave, because you would not agree to work long hours under the working time directive, because you have been a whistleblower, or demanded the national minimum wage, then you may have a case for unfair dismissal.

Think very seriously if you are offered voluntary redundancy. Ask for longer to make up your mind about a severance package, and don't be bounced into making an instant decision.

Redundancy pay

If you are made redundant in your 50s and you have been working for your employer for at least two years you will normally be entitled to statutory redundancy pay. It does not matter whether you worked full or part time. The minimum amount of redundancy pay is determined by how long you have worked for that employer and your age. You are entitled to one week's pay for each year's service aged 22 to 40 and 1½ week's pay for each year you worked from 41 to 64. The maximum years of service that can count is 20 and so the maximum entitlement is 30 weeks' pay. There is also an upper limit on what counts as a week's pay for statutory redundancy payments: £270 from February 2004. So the total statutory redundancy pay cannot be more than £8,100.

If your employer has gone bust, the Department of Trade and Industry will pay the money to you. You may also get help from the Insolvency Service.

You can get help and advice from the Insolvency Service Redundancy Payments Office on 0845 145 00 04. It will help with your rights and tell you which local Redundancy Payments Office you should be in touch with.

If your former employer is not bust but refuses to pay your redundancy money, you may have to go to an employment tribunal. Get help from your union.

Many contracts of employment specify higher amounts than the statutory minimum – a month's pay for each year's service, for example. If you are taking voluntary redundancy, the company may be prepared to pay even more as part of a package deal.

Redundancy payments are tax free up to a maximum of £30,000 but do make sure that you are made redundant properly and lawfully or the Inland Revenue may challenge the tax-free status of the payment. It may argue, for example, that your redundancy was early retirement. If it does, then appeal; mistakes are not unknown.

If you get paid more than £30,000, then the rest is taxable as income in the tax year it is received. When you leave you will also get all the wages that are owed to you, including any amounts owing for holiday pay or pay in lieu of notice. All those amounts will be taxed before you receive them. Any payment you are entitled to under your contract of employment just because you leave the company – sometimes called severance pay – is also taxable as income and will be taxed before you receive it. One way round this rule is to get any taxable money paid into your pension instead. You can then take a quarter of it out tax free and the rest will boost your pension. You can get a genuine ex gratia payment and that will not be taxable.

Losing your job late in life is a frightening thing, even if you have volunteered for it. If you hear you are going to be made redundant, take time to recover from the shock before you make any plans. Your redundancy pay may seem like a lot of tax-free cash, but it will soon disappear. So treat your new-found freedom as a time to look for new work rather than as a long paid-for holiday. Unlike most holidays, there may be no work – and little income – when the redundancy money runs out. (There is more advice on saving and investing a lump sum of money on pages 3–24.) The Age Concern book *Changing Direction* (see page 248) offers information about changing career in mid-life.

AGEISM

There is no doubt that ageism – discriminating against people on grounds of their age – is rife in the workplace. Getting a job, being retrained, gaining promotion, and keeping a job, all become more difficult once you reach 45. Of course, ageism works both ways – young people feel they are discriminated against too. One recent study found that only between the ages of 35 and 40 did people feel that their age did not cause them problems at work. But it is at the older ages that the effects of ageism really take their toll.

Between 45 and State Pension age nearly two out of every five people, 38 per cent, are economically inactive. Among younger people of working age the rate is around 26 per cent (a shade over one in four). If you do the arithmetic that could mean more than 2.5 million people over 45 would like to be at work but are not even bothering to look for a job.

There is some evidence that older workers are better employees and are likely to stay in the job for longer. An employee aged between 25 and 35 is only likely to stay in a job for 12 to 18 months. After 45 the average stay is 28 to 34 months. One study showed that the Nationwide Building Society saved £7 million in the costs of staff turnover by widening its recruitment age. Halifax, the bank, increased profits by £130,000 at six branches which used an older workforce. Older workers take less time off sick, have greater experience, a stronger work ethic and are less likely to complain. But prejudice against older workers keeps them out of the workforce. Research by the Instituto of Directors found that in half of the companies it surveyed, people over 45 represented less than one in ten of the workforce even though they make up nearly one in three of the people of working age. By 2010, they will make up almost 40 per cent of the workforce.

A survey by the Cabinet Office in 2000 estimated that ageism in employment cost the economy £16 billion a year. The Employers Forum on Age puts the cost at almost double that at £31 billion a year.

The good news is that from December 2006 it will become illegal in the UK to discriminate at work against anyone solely on grounds of age. The new law has been long resisted by the UK Government – both Conservative and Labour – but on 27 November 2000 the European Union passed a Directive to end discrimination at work on grounds of age throughout the EU. Each member state has to pass its own laws to implement the Directive. In Britain the laws will not come into force until 2 December 2006. Other EU countries started three years earlier.

Once the new law is in place it will prohibit discrimination at work (or in job-based training) on grounds of age and bring us in line with other countries including Australia, New Zealand, and the USA. Although the Government has promised that the new laws will be in place – but not in force – by the end of 2004, how tough the laws will be in the UK is still unclear. But they will almost certainly cover:

- **Recruitment** Job adverts will no longer be able to specify 'young person', 'in your 20s and eager to learn', or any of the other euphemisms that mean 'over 50s not wanted'. It will also ban discrimination the other way – adverts that specify 'mature' will not be allowed. It will be unlawful to consider age as a factor when recruiting staff.

- **Promotion** Employers will not be able to refuse promotion on grounds of age or to consider the employee's age when deciding between candidates for promotion.

- **Pay** Different rates of pay based only on age will be banned (although experience and length of service will be recognised).

- **Training** Access to training or vocational guidance will have to be given regardless of age, although there are provisions to exclude people close to retirement who would not be able to take advantage of it.

- **Redundancy** must be done on rational grounds of the needs of the employer. It should not be done to select principally older people. J Sainsbury plc, for example, has a redundancy policy that states age must not be used as a factor in redundancy decisions.

- **Retirement** Employers will not be able to fix arbitrary ages at which people will have to stop doing specific jobs or types of job. (At the time of writing it is not yet clear whether a default age of 70 will be allowed.) The do-it-yourself chain B&Q, for example, has no fixed retirement age – everyone can have phased or partial retirement when it suits them. B&Q claims that its age positive approach leads to higher productivity, reduced absences, lower turnover and improved sales.

There will be some exceptions to the rules, covering the armed forces for example, and no employer will have to keep an older person in their job if they stop being competent to do it. Employers will be able to specify a minimum age at which people can retire and draw a company pension, although the Government will try to make 65 the normal age for company schemes, by raising the normal pension age in the public sector to 65. Employers will probably not be able to force anyone to retire at a particular age and they will be able to make it financially advantageous to retire later.

These changes should be a major step towards equality for older people who want to work, although exactly how far they will go remains to be seen.

Age Positive champions are companies that have an active programme to end age discrimination against older workers. If you want to find a job, applying to one of these firms might well be a good first step. You can find a list of them on the Government's Age Positive website at www.agepositive.gov.uk (click on 'champions'). *Being Positive about Age Diversity at Work* is a government booklet which is aimed at employers but which people in their 50s looking for work may find useful. You can download a copy from www.agepositive.gov.uk

---

OTHER DISCRIMINATION

Ageism is the last of six forms of discriminations to be made unlawful. It started with the Sex Discrimination Act in 1975 and then the Race

Relations Act of 1976. It was more than 20 years later before the Disability Discrimination Act 1999 was passed. A year later the EU passed the Employment Directive on Equal Treatment which introduced three new forms of discrimination, although they are at the moment confined to work and training. In December 2003 two of them came into force in the UK – discrimination on grounds of sexual orientation, and on grounds of religion or belief. Discrimination on grounds of age will become illegal on 2 December 2006.

The Government has decided to create a new body to take over the work of the existing Commission for Racial Equality, the Equal Opportunities Commission and the Disability Rights Commission. The new body will also be responsible for the new laws outlawing workplace discrimination on grounds of age, religion or belief, and sexual orientation. It will also have a role promoting human rights – given status in UK law by the Human Rights Act 1998.

The Commission – which will probably come into existence some time in 2005 – will push forward moves which lawyers are already making to use established discrimination laws to challenge discrimination on grounds of age even before the new law comes into force. At the moment people lose all their employment rights at 65. From that age employees cannot get redundancy pay and cannot go to an employment tribunal to claim unfair dismissal. So an employer can dismiss people of that age with impunity, although legal attempts are being mounted to overturn this rule.

You can find out more about employment tribunals at the official website at www.employmenttribunals.gov.uk The Third Age Employment Network campaigns for the rights of people of all ages to work until they want to stop. You can call on 020 7843 1590 or look at the website at www.taen.org.uk The Employers Forum on Age has around 160 members (employing three million people between them). It is committed to a workforce consisting of people of all ages. You can call on 020 7981 0341 or look at the website at www.efa.org.uk The Campaign Against Age Discrimination in Employment (www.caade.net) does just what its name says.

WORKING ON

The Government has said that the State Pension will continue to be available at 65. However, it is trying to encourage people to increase the age at which they retire.

From April 2005 people who do not claim their State Pension will get a bigger enhancement to it when they do draw it. At the moment, someone who does not draw their pension gets an increment worth about 7.5 per cent for each year they defer claiming it, up to a maximum of five years. So the maximum increment is 37.5 per cent. From April 2005, if Parliament approves the proposed changes, that will be changed to an increase of 1 per cent for each five weeks of deferment – which is 10.4 per cent for each year deferred. There will be no five-year limit. So a man who finally retired at 74 and 7 months would get his State Pension doubled.

As an alternative to this enhanced pension the Government is proposing a plan which will enable you to get a lump sum instead of the higher weekly pension. In effect, it will be as if the Government was keeping your pension during the deferred period and investing it. When you draw your pension, the lump sum will be paid. Three things make this a good deal:

■ The Government will pay interest on the deferred pension of at least 6 per cent – it will be fixed at 2 percentage points above the base rate set by the Bank of England.

- The lump sum will be taxable, but only at the rate you pay on your other income. So if your income is low enough to pay no tax, then no tax will be due on it.
- The lump sum should not affect your entitlement to Pension Credit (see page 214).

The official calculations show that someone deferring the full State Pension for five years would get a lump sum of more than £23,000.

There are two problems with taking this offer:

- If you die before you take the money, only your spouse can inherit it.
- Taking the enhanced pension is a better deal – the Government says that the lump-sum option will save it money in the long run.

State Pension age for women will be raised from 60 to 65 for women retiring between 2010 and 2020. (There are more details on page 151.) Entitlement to Pension Credit, and probably the enhanced rates of other benefits, will also rise from 60 to 65 for men and women between 2010 and 2020.

The Government also wants to encourage people to work longer before they claim a pension from their employer. By 2010 the Government will raise the minimum age to claim a personal pension from 50 to 55. The minimum age for claiming an ocupational pension will also rise to 55. At the moment, the minimum is normally 50, and 62 per cent of schemes do allow retirement under 55. However, hardly any schemes have a standard pension age under 60 and seven out of ten already specify 65 for full normal benefits, although there are concessions for people over 60 in some cases. Some professions can claim their pension at a much earlier age. Those concessions will be swept away – with perhaps a few exceptions for dangerous jobs.

Civil servants and other people working in the public sector can normally retire at 60 if they choose to do so. The Government has made it clear that it wants the normal age for public servants to retire to rise to 65. It intends to introduce the change for new recruits from 2006. The change will be brought in later for existing workers, and it will only apply to the pension earned after the date of the change.

Working longer gives a double benefit to your pension. First, you (and perhaps also your employer) pay into it for longer, so there is more money in the pot when you retire. Second, you have a shorter time to live so the money you have saved will translate into a bigger pension for each year of your retirement. If you are in a scheme related to your salary, such as most public sector pensions, then your pension is related to the number of years you have paid into it. So you may get a bigger pension by working longer (check the rules of your scheme before deciding). It will also save taxpayer's money as that pension will have to be paid for a shorter time. However, the public sector at present – and a lot of private sector schemes – are currently pretty mean to people who work beyond normal retirement age, so you will need to check this out.

The details of how all this will work and how it will fit in with the new restrictions on the amount of pension that can be earned in a lifetime have yet to be announced.

Of course, not everyone wants to work after 60 or 65 – many of us are only too glad to retire after a lifetime of hard work. But as people live longer, many people are finding it tough to save enough for a decent pension. Actuaries and pension experts are predicting that people will work until they are 70 or more in future. Flexible retirement will become more important than ever.

There is also a cash boost from the Government for people who work after State Pension age (currently 60 for a woman, 65 for a man).

National Insurance contributions, which cost up to 11 per cent of your wages, are not paid by anyone over that age – a big tax break for older workers. However, the employer has to pay the same National Insurance whatever the age of their workers.

FLEXIBLE RETIREMENT

As part of its Age Positive campaign, the Government wants to discourage what it is now calling 'cliff-edge' retirement – a valued employee one day, a retired ex-employee the next. Or to put it another way, fit for work at 64, fit for nothing at 65. Instead it wants employers to introduce flexible retirement so that people can phase out their employment by working fewer hours in the day or fewer days in the week. Of course, this process does not have to start at pension age: it can start much earlier; a slow phasing out of work as both employer and employee ease themselves out of the work relationship.

There are other ways to change your working patterns to phase yourself into retirement:

- **Downshifting** Giving yourself less responsibility, perhaps moving down grades rather than up, easing the worries and pressure of the job.
- **Sabbatical** This originally meant a paid year off after seven years' employment, but now can mean any period of time on full or part pay to recharge the batteries, retrain, travel or pursue other interests.
- **Secondment** A temporary transfer to another job altogether, either within the same company or to another related organisation.
- **Volunteering** Taking some time in the working week to do tasks for a voluntary organisation; perhaps using your work skills to help a local charity, driving people to and from hospital

appointments, assisting in the local charity shop, or going abroad with VSO for example.

All of these things can help ease you out of the pressures and the nine to five routine of a normal full-time job into the rather different and freer routines of retirement. They can also help with self-esteem. Many of us define what we 'are' by the job we do. So getting another job-like activity can help ease us into a different way of seeing things.

One of the big barriers to flexible retirement is the current rule that forbids someone from drawing a pension from an occupational scheme and working for the same employer. You can draw your pension and go and work for another firm, but not change to part-time work or a different job for the same company. Relaxing this rule is one of the changes the Government plans to introduce in April 2006.

These schemes do not suit everyone. You have to consider if you can afford the drop in income. If you earn less, you will probably be paying less into your pension, so it could cut your income in retirement as well. But if you can afford it, then psychologically it can be much better to phase yourself out of work than suddenly be working full time one day and having nothing to do the next. It is also an opportunity to sort out the changes in home life. Whether you live alone or with someone, it will be very different to do without the structure of going to work each day.

Early retirement on health grounds

If your work, or travelling to it, is getting too onerous, you may want to consider early retirement. Some pension schemes – usually the salary-related ones and especially in the public sector – have special rules for people whose health deteriorates in their 50s to allow them to retire early with little or no loss of pension benefits, although you may not be able to draw them immediately. You should ask your employer if your scheme has such rules.

If you are in a money purchase pension, then the rules are likely to be completely unhelpful – you stop contributing early, so you get a lower pension.

DISABILITY

One of the less pleasant aspects of reaching your 50s is a sense that your body is not as energetic, or supple or capable as it once was. These things creep up slowly but there comes a time when you run for a bus, try to kick a ball, or need to paint the ceiling and you suddenly think – I am getting older. These changes happen to everyone, even those who are fit and healthy. But for some people in their 50s it goes beyond that – ageing turns to disability. A hard working life, an accident or an illness can all lead to a disability that can enable you to get extra help from the Department for Work and Pensions. It is hard to admit that the persistent pain in your back or the old injury on your knee which you have lived with for years has now become a disability.

If you are still at work, you may want to talk to your employer about early retirement on health grounds (see above). Some occupational pensions – especially in the public sector – do offer good terms to people in these circumstances.

DISCRIMINATION

If you feel you are disabled and it affects your ability to work, then it can lead to a more sympathetic treatment by the Department for

Work and Pensions. Remember too that under the Disability Discrimination Act 1995 it can be illegal to treat disabled people less favourably than others. You can be counted as disabled if you have a mental or physical impairment that has a substantial and long-term adverse effect on your ability to carry out normal day-to-day activities.

From 1 October 2004 the Disability Discrimination Act (DDA) extends to many parts of life including:

Work If you are disabled, or have had a disability, the DDA makes it unlawful for an employer who employs 15 or more people to discriminate against you when you are applying for a job or are in work. If such discrimination does exist, then an employer has to take 'reasonable steps' to end it. You cannot be dismissed or made redundant just because you have a disability, although of course if your disability means that you can no longer do your job, and that reasonable steps by the employer cannot mitigate that inability, then it is possible that you might lose your job. The employer must first try to find you a suitable alternative job within the company. Clearly, that is easier for a large employer to do than a smaller one.

Goods and services Shops, restaurants and other retails outlets, public buildings such as libraries, and offices that are open to the public, have to make sure that disabled people can access them and have equal access to the goods or services they provide.

Health and education Providers must ensure equal access to health services and education facilities regardless of disability.

If you believe that any disability is leading to discrimination against you, get help and advice from the Disability Rights Commission on 08457 622 633 or at www.drc-gb.org

---

DISABILITY BENEFITS

Social security benefits for disabled people are very complex and this book can only give a very brief guide to them.

You can get more information from the Department for Work and Pensions website at www.dwp.gov.uk (click on 'disabled people and carers' to go to many pages of advice and help). You can also find out about disability and get advice about benefits and campaigning from the Disability Alliance on 020 7247 8776 or at www.disabilityalliance.org The Disability Alliance publishes *The Disability Rights Handbook*, which is a comprehensive guide to disability rights and benefits.

Statutory Sick Pay

If you have a job and are ill so that you cannot work, then you will normally get Statutory Sick Pay (SSP). Most employers will give you full pay for a period of time. But if your employer will not, or that period of time comes to an end, then SSP is paid. It is not paid for the first three days of sickness. It can last up to 28 weeks. It is £66.16 a week in 2004–2005 and is paid by your employer. You cannot get SSP if you earn less than £79 a week.

Incapacity Benefit

Incapacity Benefit is paid if you are too ill to work and do not get Statutory Sick Pay. That may be because you earn too little, your employer cannot or does not pay you SSP (although an employer has a legal obligation to do so, some may not for various reasons), you have lost your job, you are self-employed, or your SSP has run out.

To get Incapacity Benefit you must have paid enough full National Insurance contributions – either Class 1 as employed or Class 2 as self-employed. Normally that will mean you have paid the contributions in one of the last three tax years before the calendar year in which you fall ill.

Incapacity Benefit is paid at three different rates depending how long your incapacity has lasted:

Short-term lower rate	First 28 weeks of incapacity	£55.90
Short-term higher rate	From 29–52 weeks of incapacity	£66.15
Long-term rate	More than 52 weeks of incapacity	£74.15

You can get extra amounts if you have an adult dependant such as a wife or husband who does not work (although generally, unless you have a dependent child, they must be aged 60 or over). Your Incapacity Benefit will be reduced if you have a personal or occupational pension which is more than £85 a week. It will be cut by half the amount of your pension over £85 a week. So if your pension is £105, your Incapacity Benefit will be cut by £10 (£105 minus £85 = £20; £20 ÷ 2 = £10).

You should claim Incapacity Benefit as soon as you think you may have a claim because it can only be backdated by three months. Claim on the form from the DWP website or from a local Jobcentre Plus office.

Disability Living Allowance

If your disability becomes very severe and you need help from someone else with your daily life then you may be entitled to Disability Living Allowance (DLA). It gives you extra money to help with the costs of getting around and personal care. It is a benefit for people aged under 65 when they claim it (Attendance Allowance is a similar benefit for those aged 65 or over but is more limited in the help it provides).

DLA is tax free and is paid on top of other benefits and pensions. In fact, you may be entitled to claim extra benefits, so ask for advice if you start to get DLA, or the amount you get is increased.

DLA is divided into two parts:

- **care component** – for people who need help from others to cope with their personal care and daily living tasks; and
- **mobility component** – for people who have difficulty in walking or getting around.

You can qualify for either the care component or the mobility component separately, or you can qualify for both.

Care component

You can claim the care component of DLA if you need help with personal care from another person. You do not have to be actually getting help from anyone already. What is important is that you need help. You must normally have needed this help for the three months immediately before you claim and you must expect to need help for the six months afterwards.

There are three rates of care component according to how much help you need:

Highest rate – £58.80 per week
Middle rate – £39.35 per week
Lowest rate – £15.55 per week

Which rate you get depends on how much care you need from someone else.

For the **lowest rate** you must need attention from another person to deal with some 'bodily function' for more than an hour a day. Alternatively, you must be unable to cook a main meal for yourself if you have the ingredients. It doesn't matter if you do not normally cook – what is important is whether you would be able to safely carry out the tasks normally involved in cooking such as peeling, chopping, lifting, using the cooker or taps.

The **highest rate** is paid if you need help during the day and the night. The **middle rate** is paid if you need help either during the day or during the night.

To qualify **by day** you must need frequent attention throughout the day in connection with your bodily functions. 'Throughout the day' means in the middle of the day as well as in the morning and evening, but it does not have to be all day or indeed every day – it is the pattern of care needed over a period of time which is important. Your bodily functions are things like eating, preparing meals, using the toilet, getting up, washing and dressing, taking medication or using a wheelchair. It also means walking and other physical activities that allow you to carry out a reasonable level of social, recreational or leisure activity. Blind or deaf people who need help with daily tasks because of their lack of sight or hearing may now qualify.

Alternatively, you can qualify if you need continual supervision throughout the day to avoid substantial danger to yourself or others. The supervision needs to be 'continual', even if the reason for it may only occur occasionally. For example, people who are likely to have an epileptic fit or who have dementia or other mental problems may only put themselves at risk occasionally, but the supervision has to be continual because they may have a fit or a dangerous spell at any time. The 'substantial danger' must be likely, but it need never have actually happened.

To qualify **by night** you must need prolonged or repeated attention in connection with your bodily functions. 'Prolonged' means for a period of 20 minutes or more. 'Repeated' means more than once.

211

Alternatively, you must need another person to be awake for a prolonged period or at frequent intervals for the purpose of watching over you to avoid substantial danger to yourself or others.

Mobility component

You can claim the mobility component of DLA if you have difficulty walking or getting about. You must normally have had mobility problems for the three months immediately before you claim and expect to have the same difficulties for the six months afterwards.

There are two rates of mobility component:

Higher rate – £41.05 per week
Lower rate – £15.55 per week

To qualify for the **higher rate**, you must be unable to walk, or have great difficulty walking, or be in serious danger if you do walk. In all cases your ability to walk is considered using any artificial limbs or aids which you normally use. If you can walk but find that doing so causes you severe pain or discomfort, or if you are very limited in the distance you can walk, or the speed you can walk, or the time you can walk for, then you should qualify for the higher rate.

You can qualify for the **lower rate** of mobility component even if you can walk. To get the lower rate, you must need guidance or supervision from someone else to make sure you are safe or to help you find your way around in a strange place.

An organisation called Motability (address on page 240) helps people use the highest rate of mobility component to purchase or lease a suitable vehicle. However, your DLA may not cover all the costs; you may have to pay a deposit or for the cost of adaptations and you will have to pay the running costs. Do check exactly what you will need to pay before committing yourself.

War Disablement Pension

Some men in their late 50s may have been called up for National Service. Other men and women in their 50s will be ex-service people. Any disability suffered now which has its roots in the period of service in the armed forces may bring entitlement to a benefit misleadingly called War Disablement Pension. Anyone who served in the forces, including National Service, and suffered an injury or disease as a result may be entitled to this pension. It is not means tested and is tax free.

You can find out more from the Veterans Agency on 0800 169 22 77 or at www.veteransagency.mod.uk and you can get advice and assistance from the Royal British Legion on its Legion Line on 08457 725 725 or its website at www.britishlegion.org.uk

---

Income Support

The main means-tested benefit for people who do not work and have a low income is Income Support. If you are capable of work then normally you will have to be actively looking for a job and claim Jobseeker's Allowance. But if you cannot work, perhaps because of disability or being a lone parent or a carer, then you may be able to claim Income Support. How much you get will depend on your other income and your savings as well as your personal and family circumstances.

Income Support brings your income up to £55.65 in 2004–2005 if you are single or £87.30 for a couple (both of you must have a good reason why you cannot work). If you have a disability you can get more than these amounts. If you have savings of more than £3,000 your Income Support will be reduced, and if you have more than £8,000 then you cannot get Income Support.

Income Support applies to people under the age of 60. Once you reach 60 the rules change dramatically. Firstly, you are no longer required to work or to seek work. That rule applies equally to men and women, even though the State Pension age for men is 65 and between 2010 and 2020 it is rising to that age for women (see page 151). Secondly, you do not get Income Support; instead you can claim Pension Credit. That brings your income up to £105.45 a week in 2004–2005 if you are single or £160.95 between them for a couple and there is no upper limit on savings. So at age 59 and 11 months the Government thinks you need £55.65 a week to keep body and soul together, but a few weeks later, once you reach 60, the weekly amount you need jumps to £105.45, nearly twice as much. Pension Credit levels go up each year in line with earnings while Income Support (and Jobseeker's Allowance) goes up with prices. As earnings rise more than prices, if the current uprating policy continues, it will not be many years before someone in their 50s gets half the money paid to a 60 year old. At 65, Pension Credit is worth still more to many people.

FROM CAREER TO CARER

Just as disability creeps upon us as we get older, so does caring. In our 50s it often happens that parents or other older relatives become dependent on others for their care and happiness. Who takes on that responsibility is often a matter of chance. Many people at first combine it with a full-time job, but find that becomes more and more difficult and finally impossible.

The value of carers is not properly recognised in the UK. An estimated 6 million people give regular care to a relative or friend. Yet only around 400,000 people get any sort of financial assistance from the State for doing so – and women outnumber men by three to one. At some point in our life three out of five of us will become a carer.

Carer's Allowance

If you look after someone who is disabled you may be entitled to Carer's Allowance (which used to be called Invalid Care Allowance). But there are many conditions surrounding it. Normally you have to give 35 hours care each week in order to claim Carer's Allowance. However, once you have been caring for someone for six months you do not lose the benefit if you have up to four weeks off in any six-month period.

To get Carer's Allowance you normally cannot earn more than £79 a week from work, either as an employee or self-employed, nor can you get it if you are in full-time education. There is no upper age limit, although you cannot get Carer's Allowance on top of some other benefits such as the State Pension.

The person you are caring for must normally be claiming the higher or middle rate of Disability Living Allowance care component (see pages 209–212), Attendance Allowance (which is a similar benefit for people aged 65 or over), or Constant Attendance Allowance (which is a similar benefit for people who have an Industrial or War Disablement Pension). The person you are caring for can be anyone, including a relative or spouse. It is even possible for two spouses to receive it, each caring for the other.

Carer's Allowance is not enough to live on – it is just £44.35 a week in 2004–2005. However, if you get it, then you may also claim Income Support (see pages 213–214) without having to worry about looking for work. Carer's Allowance also brings with it entitlement to higher rates of Housing Benefit and Council Tax Benefit. You can also get help with qualifying for a full Basic State Pension, and to increase the amount of State Second Pension you will receive, through Home Responsibilities Protection (see page 150).

You can get more information or make a claim by calling the Carer's Allowance Helpline on 01772 899729. You can get more information or claim online at the DWP website at www.dwp.gov.uk

HELP WITH CARING

Your local council can help you with information and practical services. As a carer you have a right to an assessment by the social services department of your local council. The assessment will look at what you need as a carer, although whether the social services department will have the money or ability to provide the services or help you need is another matter.

If you are working and caring, you do have limited rights to 'reasonable' time off to help people who are dependent on you.

You can get more information about assessments for carers and carers' rights from Carers UK on 0808 808 7777 or at www.carersonline.org.uk Carers UK will also be able to tell you if there is a carers' support group locally.

RELATIONSHIP BREAKDOWN

The ending of a relationship is something a growing number of people in their 50s have to face. Divorces among 50-somethings are rising. Although the total number of divorces fell by more than 9 per cent between 1991 and 2001, among people aged 45 and more the numbers rose. That is especially true for people in their 50s – up by 40 per cent for men and by 50 per cent for women over that ten-year period. In 2001, more than 20,000 men (1 in 12) and nearly

16,000 women (1 in 15) in their 50s divorced. There is no age breakdown of the nearly four million people who live in an unmarried couple, but they form around 1 in 12 of all households. It is reasonable to assume that their relationships are also breaking down more than before.

DIVORCE

Marriage carries with it legal consequences and financial obligations and these have to be put asunder on divorce. In the USA pre-nuptial agreements which protect assets acquired before the marriage are popular and have legal effect. In the UK the courts have held them to be ineffective.

Children complicate matters but in your 50s you are less likely to have dependent offspring. Most people who divorce in their 50s want what is called a 'clean break' – in other words, after the divorce they will not depend on each other financially in the future. At the divorce, they split their jointly-owned property and go their separate ways. Broadly speaking, a wife and husband separate their assets equally, regardless of who brought what to the marriage or who contributed most financially during it.

On divorce the courts will look at all your assets – your home, savings and investments, valuables and property, any business you jointly own, and the pension rights of each partner. Splitting savings, investments, valuables, and movable property is normally quite straightforward, but do remember that three chairs each are worth a lot less than a set of six to one partner.

The assets that are hardest to deal with are your home and your pension rights – and any business which you may share. You will also find how true is the old saying that two can live as cheaply as one.

217

Separated couples will need two washing machines, two televisions, perhaps two cars, and, of course, two places to live.

Your home

Your home may have to be sold. It is worth trying everything you can to avoid that, however, and keep it for the financially weaker partner. The one – or two – left without a home in their 50s may have problems in buying a replacement. First, you may have only a small share of the value of the original home. Second, if you have to arrange a mortgage, lenders will assume that you will stop working at 65 if you are an employee or 70 if you are self-employed. That means that a repayment mortgage will be an expensive option with far less than the normal period to repay the loan. You could consider an interest-only mortgage, relying perhaps on a pension lump sum, an inheritance, or good fortune to repay the capital. You need to be confident and a good sleeper to be able to do that.

Lenders will also want to be sure that you have the income to meet the repayments. Normally maintenance payments from your ex-husband or wife will not be counted as income – unless they are secured by a court order and you are borrowing less than 75 per cent of the value of the property. It is also difficult for one partner to get a mortgage on a new property if they also have a remaining mortgage on the first. You need a good mortgage broker to sort these problems out.

If you remarry, remember that any will you have made prior to that remarriage will be invalid and has to be remade or it will be of no effect. Also remember that a new spouse will immediately acquire rights to your property, including property your children may at some stage expect to inherit. If you die and then your new spouse marries again, the property could end up a long way from your original family.

Your pension

The right to a pension is a very valuable asset. In a marriage it is normally assumed that the pension will provide, at least partly, for both partners. But it is only fairly recently that its value has formed a separate and divisible part of the assets to be shared between the partners.

There are three ways a pension can be shared. All of them require that the rights to the pension should be valued, and that is normally done by asking for a Cash Equivalent Transfer Value (CETV). The pension fund or insurance company has to provide that to the court. The value of each partner's pension should be counted by the court as an asset on each side. Remember that public sector jobs (including teachers, nurses, and civil servants) bring with them valuable salary-related pensions, so an apparently economically weaker partner can nevertheless have valuable rights to a future pension. For example, a woman who earns much less than her husband may find that the value of her public sector pension is more than the value of his money purchase or personal pension that has no guarantees with it.

Once the value has been obtained, there are three ways it can be split:

■ **Its value can simply be counted as part of the assets to be split.** One party may keep the whole of the pension as long as the other gets assets of an equivalent value. For example, if the CETV of the pension was £100,000 and the marital home was also valued at £100,000, one partner could have the house and the other the pension. This method is called 'offsetting'. Usually, however, it is not so neat, although it is still the most common way of dealing with the problem and can be the most straightforward.

■ **It can be 'earmarked'** – that means that when the person with the pension rights reaches the scheme's pension age, the scheme pays a pension both to them and to their ex-spouse. Earmarking began in 1996 but its limitations were soon realised and it is seldom used.

■ **Pension splitting** – this is a more straightforward method which began for divorces granted from 1 December 2000. Once the CETV has been obtained, then if no other division of the assets would produce a fair settlement, the pension itself can be split. For example, if a husband had an occupational pension which provided him with a pension of £25,000 a year, index-linked, as well as a widows' pension and a lump sum, then a value would be put on this (probably around £500,000) and the pension fund would have to transfer half of that sum to a pension in his ex-wife's name. She would have to use it to buy a pension herself from a pension provider.

These deals can be very complex and the ideal, of course, is for both parties to come to an amicable agreement – with the help of their solicitors – and leave the courts out of it. Pension splitting and the CETV do help achieve a result that is genuinely fair to both parties, however. Pension splitting remains rare, and is not suitable for pensions that are not very valuable.

Many solicitors are not very good at the complex calculations involved in splitting assets, especially pensions. You can find out lawyers who specialise in amicable and efficient divorces through the Solicitors Family Law Association. It has more than 5,000 registered solicitors. Contact the Association at www.sfla.org.uk or call 01689 850227.

Your State Pension

The SERPS or S2P part of a State Pension (see pages 154–156) is dealt with in the same way as an occupational or personal pension and can be split along the lines set out above on pages 219–220. The Basic State Pension is treated differently. Once you are divorced, each partner can use the other's National Insurance contributions instead of their own, either for their whole working life or for the time they were married. Usually this means that a woman who has an inadequate National Insurance contribution record can get a full record and a full pension. So make sure that the Inland Revenue and the Department for Work and Pensions knows about your divorce so that advice about your pension entitlement – and, of course, the pension you eventually draw – is correct. (There is more about National Insurance contributions on pages 148–149.)

If you remarry before State Pension age, you lose the right to use your former spouse's contribution record. However, once you have reached State Pension age and claimed your State Pension based on your former spouse's contributions, the pension is not taken away if you marry. So if you are divorced, it may be worth considering putting off remarriage until you have reached State Pension age and claimed your pension.

| SEPARATION |

For most financial arrangements separation has no real effect. A separated wife and husband are still married and their tax position and financial obligations remain much the same. The one exception is entitlement to means-tested benefits and tax credits. They are calculated on joint income for opposite sex couples who live together, married or not. Separated people who live alone have their own income counted separately, although if you have dependent children then the Child Support Agency will get involved and try to obtain a contribution from the absent father or mother.

An occupational pension will still be paid to the person who has earned it. The separated partner will still have rights to a pension as a widow or widower when their separated partner dies.

You will still be treated as married when your Basic State Pension is worked out. So if you are a married woman with no rights to a pension yourself, then you will just get the married woman's pension, which is £44.35 in 2004–2005, instead of the full pension of £79.60. So if you are separated, you may want to consider divorce – it can boost your income and it may give you other rights to half your spouse's property.

SAME SEX COUPLES

The Government has announced its intention to allow same sex couples to make a declaration of their commitment and to enter into a 'civil partnership'. These relationships will bring most of the rights and responsibilities of marriage, and will have to be dissolved by the courts. The new law could come into effect by the end of 2005. Civil partners will have the same rights and benefits in tax and social security as married couples. Couples of different sexes will not be able to register a civil partnership, but they can get married.

UNMARRIED COUPLES

More and more people live together without getting married and this is, of course, true of people in their 50s as well as younger people. Marriage is less popular than it has ever been. In 2001 it hit its lowest point since 1897. It rose slightly in 2002 when there were just under

300,000 weddings in the UK. Almost half of those were remarriages. Thirty years earlier in 1972 there were almost half a million weddings. That means a lot of couples are living in a financially insecure relationship.

Women in particular should be aware that living together confers no financial rights whatsoever. You can live with someone for years, decorate their home, cook their meals, and have their children, without gaining a single financial right to their property – including the home you share – if it is 'his' rather than 'yours'. That can come as a major shock when the relationship breaks down. So marriage gives much more security for the financially weaker partner. It is worth remembering that when a new relationship is formed.

MOVING ABROAD

Many of us have a fantasy at some point of giving it all up and moving abroad. Our 50s can be just the time when it seems right to try to turn those dreams into reality. But there is a lot to consider before you sell up and commit yourself to living abroad for the rest of your life. Many people have lost much of their money and found themselves returning to the UK with their tail between their legs, poorer and not much wiser, than when they left. So it is something to be thought about very carefully before you do it. This book can only give some pointers about the difficulties and advantages, and where to find more information.

MAKING THE DECISION

People want to live abroad for many reasons. A warmer climate can mean better health. Cheaper property can mean a nicer home or spare cash to boost retirement income. Better – and cheaper – food and drink, as well as lower prices on clothes and other goods and services, mean a better standard of living. Culture and history may seem to be more beautiful or interesting. Sports and leisure activities can be more fun in the sun. Sometimes it is as simple as being able to have a nice breakfast on a sunny terrace every morning. Some of these dreams are illusions – what can seem great for a few weeks on holiday can disappear rapidly if it is the whole of your life. On the other hand, rainy and expensive Britain can seem a miserable place to pass the last stages of your life.

Remember, however, that there are great disadvantages in moving permanently to another country. You will leave behind family and friends, and all those promises to come and see you will be even harder to fulfil abroad than they are elsewhere in the UK. Without those contacts you may feel isolated or even bored. Don't forget too that if you make this change with your spouse or partner, one of you will eventually be left alone there. In many parts of the world – even in Europe – you will not find a free health service or even one of comparable quality at any price. You may be healthy in your 50s, but make sure that you can cope with illness or disability in your 70s or 80s. You will have to cope with another legal system and an entirely foreign bureaucracy; and usually do that in a foreign language. The culture you loved so much on holidays may seem strange, old-fashioned, peculiar, stupid or even frightening when you have to live among it. Public transport may be difficult or non-existent. So make sure that the place you choose is somewhere you want to live, not just somewhere you have had great holidays.

In addition to these general considerations, there are legal and financial consequences to be aware of. In the fifteen member states of the old European Union there should not be any problems about staying permanently as a retired resident. But the ten new countries which joined in May 2004 may impose some restrictions until 2011. It is vital to check first. Anywhere else in the world may – and most likely does – impose restrictions on foreign nationals settling and retiring. Many demand a family connection or a certain (usually large) amount of money to be allowed to settle. In others you may find it is simply impossible to be guaranteed permanent residence.

STATE BENEFITS

Most State benefits are not paid to you if you live permanently abroad. The major exception is war pensions – both for disablement and widows. They are paid anywhere in the world at the rate they are paid in the UK, although extra amounts for constant attendance and exceptionally severe disablement are not paid abroad.

State Pension (but not Pension Credit) and bereavements benefits can be paid abroad but they are subject to special rules. In most countries they are not increased each year in line with inflation. Instead, they are frozen at the rate you were first paid the pension abroad. The exceptions to this rule are the 25 countries of the European Union, the three countries which are in the European Economic Area but not in the EU, and 20 other countries with which Britain has a special agreement. (These countries are listed in the Appendix on page 244.) More than half the expatriate pensioner population lives outside these countries. If you get a State Pension and go abroad to live – or for more than six months – you must tell the Department for Work and Pensions.

Your pension can:

■   be paid into a bank account abroad, although it will be paid in Sterling and you will be responsible for the cost of conversion into the local currency;

225

- continue to be paid into a bank account in the UK in Sterling and you will be responsible for converting it into local currency when you need it; or
- you can get an order posted to you, which you will have to pay into a local bank, again meeting the conversion charges.

None of the income-related benefits can be paid abroad – including Income Support, Pension Credit, Housing Benefit and any tax credits. In the EU you should be able to claim local income-related benefits. But few countries have a means-tested social security system anything like ours. So if you rely on those benefits in the UK, you may well end up with a lower income if you live abroad.

Apart from War Disablement Pension, disability benefits cannot generally be paid if you have moved permanently to another country, although some may be paid for up to 26 weeks of temporary absence, especially if you are going abroad for treatment related to your disability.

You can get more information from the Centre for Non-Residents (CNR) Helpline on 084591 54811 or the International Pension Centre on 0191 218 7777.

NATIONAL INSURANCE

If you are under 60 you can pay National Insurance contributions to make sure you get a full State Pension when you retire. Whether that is worth doing depends on how much State Pension you have already earned. If you have already paid enough contributions to get a full State Pension, then there is no point in paying any extra – and no point either once you are 60 or more as credits are given automatically if you need them. But if paying more would give you a bigger pension then it may be worthwhile. So get a State Pension forecast and decide if it is worth paying more and for how many years. (See pages 151–154 for more details on paying voluntary National Insurance contributions and the effect they have.)

You can get a forecast or find out more from The Pension Service website at www.thepensionservice.gov.uk or by calling 0845 3000 168. More information is provided in Inland Revenue leaflet NI38 *Social Security Abroad*, which also contains a form to fill in if you want to pay National Insurance contributions while you are abroad. DWP Leaflet SA29 *Your Social Security Insurance, Benefits and Healthcare Rights in the European Economic Area* also contains a lot of useful information.

If you work in a foreign country then you will probably be paying into the local state pension system and, depending how long you work, you may be able to draw a local pension when you reach the pension age for that country.

OCCUPATIONAL OR PERSONAL PENSION

A pension or annuity from your job, or one you have paid into yourself, can be paid abroad. If your pension or annuity is normally increased each year then that will continue. However, your pension or annuity will be paid in Sterling and you will be responsible for the cost of converting it into the local currency. That also means that your actual income will vary with the exchange rate. Lots of small payments will mean paying a lot of bank charges. If you have several small pensions, it may be worth keeping a UK account to receive them all and then making one transfer to the country where you live.

TAX

The first thing you have to decide is – where do you live? There are very strict and complicated rules about which country you pay tax in if you move from one to another. This section assumes that you are moving permanently to live in another country and will not spend more than a quarter of each year back in the UK. In those circumstances you stop being both 'resident' and 'ordinarily resident' in the UK. When that happens you stop having to pay tax on any income that arises outside the UK. So any money you earn or make while living abroad is not taxable in the UK. It may, of course, be taxable in the country where you now live.

Income that arises in the UK may still in theory be taxable in the UK. So any interest paid on a UK savings account or on gilts, any dividends paid on UK shares or investments, any pension or annuity paid by a UK pension fund or insurance company, and any rental income from property in the UK, are all potentially taxable in the UK.

Two things limit the tax that can be charged on income arising in the UK. First, most people – including all British citizens and citizens of any other Commonwealth country – are still entitled to a personal tax allowance against their UK income before tax is due. So, in 2004–2005, the first £4,745 of income is not taxed. Second, the UK has a double taxation agreement with most countries. These agreements normally provide for your income from a pension and investments in the UK to be taxed in the country where you live. In that case the interest and the pension can be paid gross, without deduction of UK tax. You will have to tell the pension provider, and the bank or building society where your money is deposited, about your non-resident status. However, any income from rent on a UK property is always taxed in the UK. The Rent a Room scheme (see pages

184–185) does not apply if you are not resident. You can, however, set the profit from your rental against your UK personal allowance.

The position is complicated and you should seek advice from an accountant or your local tax enquiry office before you go abroad. Even when you do go abroad you will be liable to pay all the UK tax up to the date of departure: normally if you leave after 6 October then you will be taxed for the whole of the tax year in which you leave.

Residence and ordinary residence are quite easy things to define. Much harder is the concept of 'domicile'. Everyone has a domicile of birth which is the same domicile as that of their father. Once you reach 16 you can change your domicile by moving permanently to another country. So if you retire abroad and intend to stay there until you die, then that country may become your domicile of choice. However, if you intend to stay for a long time in a country but still keep property or connections in another country, say the UK, then you will not acquire domicile in your new country. Domicile can affect the way you are taxed on income and capital gains, and it is most likely to affect your will and liability to Inheritance Tax.

If you spend part of the year abroad – perhaps because you have a second home to spend the winter in – you will normally be counted as resident and domiciled in the UK and have to pay tax here. How the other country treats you will depend on local laws.

Taxes on wealth

Remember that you will be subject to wealth and inheritance tax in the country where you become resident. Both Spain and France have a wealth tax and almost all countries have inheritance taxes. You should make sure you understand – and are happy with – these taxes for the country where you are planning to settle. In particular, check on the position of husbands and wives. The UK rule that transfers between spouses are free of tax may not apply abroad. You should also let your heirs know what they will have to do when they finally come to sort out your financial affairs.

Make sure you understand the local laws about wills. You should always make a will locally to deal with your property in the country where you are living. In many countries you cannot disinherit blood relatives in the way you can in the UK. Property outside that country may be dealt with separately, particularly if you do not establish 'domicile' in your new country. If you do not make a will, then sorting out your financial affairs may be very difficult for those you leave behind.

BUYING PROPERTY

Buying a house or flat in the UK can be stressful enough. In another country, with a different legal system and a foreign language, it can be much worse. Even when it all goes well, there can be problems in continental Europe about exactly what title you have to the property and what rights others may have over your property. Local lawyers can be slipshod about such things and it is often much harder abroad to get any compensation.

In Spain in particular many British expats have bought their dream home only to find it turn into a nightmare. In the worst cases they have had to pay out very large sums of money to developers building roads or drains nearby for new developments. Some have ended up owing so much they have lost their home. Others have been surprised to discover that they are liable for the debts of the previous owner – not just for missed mortgage payments, but even for speeding fines. Many prospective owners have been shocked to be asked for up to 25 per cent extra on top of the price in cash so the vendor can avoid the high taxes on property sales.

You should be very careful too when buying new property. You are often asked to buy before the foundations have been dug and are rushed into a decision with no time to get advice or consider things carefully. Even when things go well, many new developments may be suitable as holiday homes but are just not up to the job of being your own home to live in all the year round. It is usually better to find an established home that a local family has lived in and buy that, as you would in the UK.

Remember that just about every country has some sort of tax or charge on property. Make sure you know what you are letting yourself in for.

If you borrow money locally to buy the property but your income is still in Sterling, as it will normally be, then you run the extra risk of the exchange rate moving in the wrong direction, leaving you with a bigger bill. If you find the payments are hard to repay, local laws may allow far more draconian methods to recover the money than they do here.

All these dangers and difficulties make it essential to have an escape route back home – at least for a while. So if you can afford to move abroad without selling your home here, then that is ideal. One way is to let out your home so that you can try out the new country and give yourself time to be sure you have avoided the legal and financial pitfalls. (See pages 58–63 for details about letting your home.) But remember that any rental income from your property will still be taxable in the UK (see page 228).

If you do return to the UK, then remember that you will be considered resident here for the whole tax year if you arrive before 6 October.

The Age Concern Books publication *Retiring to Spain* (see page 248) has more information about all aspects of moving to Spain.

MOTORING

If you are taking your UK registered car with you, check how long you can keep it in the foreign country without re-registering it there. Check if you need a driving licence – although tourists are covered by their home licence, it is a different matter if you become a resident. Make sure too, of course, that the vehicle is insured – again, your UK insurance will not cover you once you are settled in another country and may not fully cover you or cover you at all without making arrangements before you leave. These things may seem obvious but are easy to overlook. The positive side is that sorting them out will help you understand not just the local language but the bureaucracy and the way things work. Remember too that driving laws can be very different; in particular, many countries outside the UK have stricter laws on driving after drinking alcohol.

HEALTH

Although we complain about the National Health Service, most of us are very glad of it from time to time. In particular, the NHS is almost unsurpassed for the treatment you get for urgent life-threatening conditions and is pretty well unique in being free at the point of need. In most other countries health services have to be paid for; either directly, through a specific tax or charge, or through compulsory or voluntary health insurance. So remember to check carefully with the country where you are going to live. Make sure that you are happy with the quality of the health care service and that you build in the cost of either the local taxes or of private health care insurance. Remember too that as you get older those costs might rise considerably.

In some countries you will be expected to take a family member with you to hospital to attend to your personal needs, such as feeding and going to the toilet – nurses may only provide nursing care. You may also find that you are discharged back home more quickly than you are in the UK.

If you are travelling to a country in the EU or the EEA (see the Appendix on page 244), you can get information about the health system there from DWP leaflet SA29 *Your Social Security Insurance, Benefits and Healthcare Rights in the European Economic Area.*

FURTHER
INFORMATION

This final section details national addresses you can contact for assistance and advice. The uprating countries are listed in the appendix, and there is also an index to help you find the information you need in the book.

USEFUL ADDRESSES

Association of British Insurers (ABI)

51 Gresham Street

London EC2V 7HQ

Tel: 020 7600 3333

Website: www.abi.org.uk

Offers advice and information on a wide range of insurance products. Runs a quality standard scheme called Raising Standards which assesses financial services products – see the website www.raisingstandards.net for more information.

Association of Residential Letting Agents (ARLA)

Maple House

53–55 Woodside Road

Amersham

Bucks HP6 6AA

Tel: 0845 345 5752

Website: www.arla.co.uk/btl

For information about Buy to Let.

Banking Code Standards Board

33 St James's Square

London SW1Y 4JS

Tel: 020 7661 9694

Website: www.bankingcode.org.uk

For information about protection for money in bank and building society accounts.

British Bankers' Association Dormant Accounts Scheme

Dormant Accounts Unit

The British Bankers' Association

Pinners Hall

105–108 Old Broad Street

London EC2N 1EX

Tel: 020 7216 8909

Website: www.bba.org.uk

Will help you if you are trying to track down an old bank account.

Building Societies Association Dormant Account Scheme

Building Societies Association

3 Savile Row

London W1S 3PB

Tel: 020 7437 0655

Website: www.bsa.org.uk

Will help you if you are trying to track down an old building society account.

Call Credit

Consumer Service Department

Park Row House

Leeds LS1 5JF

Tel: 0870 060 1414

Website: www.callcredit.plc.uk

A new credit reference company.

CareHealth Ltd

19 Hampden Hill

Beaconsfield

Buckinghamshire HP9 1BP

Tel: 01494 680202

Tel: www.carehealth.co.uk

For information about the cost of common operations and medical insurance.

Carers UK

20–25 Glasshouse Yard

London EC1A 4JT

Tel: 020 7490 8818 (admin)
CarersLine: 0808 808 7777
Website: www.carersonline.org.uk
Provides general advice and help for all carers.

Consumer Credit Counselling Service
Wade House
Merrion Centre
Leeds LS2 8NG
Tel: 0800 138 1111
Website: www.cccs.co.uk
For advice if you have debt problems.

Debt Management Office (DMO)
Eastcheap Court
11 Philpot Lane
London EC3M 8UD
Tel: 020 7862 6500
Website: www.dmo.gov.uk
Administers gilts for the Government and produces a free guide for private investors.

Disability Alliance
Universal House
88–94 Wentworth Street
London E1 7SA
Tel: 020 7247 8776
Rights Advice Line: 020 7247 8763 (2pm–4pm, Mondays and Wednesdays)
Website: www.disabilityalliance.org
Produces the Disability Rights Handbook *and other publications and gives advice on social security benefits for disabled people through the Rights Advice Line.*

Disability Rights Commission
DRC Helpline
FREEPOST MID02164
Stratford upon Avon CV37 9BR
Tel: 08457 622 633
Website: www.drc-gb.org
For information about the rights of disabled people.

Equifax Plc
Credit File Advice Centre
PO Box 1140
Bradford BD1 5US
Tel: 0845 600 1772
Website: www.equifax.co.uk
One of the major credit reference agencies.

Experian Ltd
Consumer Help Service
PO Box 8000
Nottingham NG1 5GX
Tel: 0870 2416212
Website: www.uk.experian.com
One of the major credit reference agencies.

Financial Ombudsman Service (FOS)
South Quay Plaza
183 Marsh Wall
London E14 9SR
Consumer Helpline: 0845 080 1800
Website: www.financial-ombudsman.org.uk
Provides consumers with a free independent service for resolving disputes with financial firms.

The Financial Services Authority (FSA)

25 The North Colonnade

Canary Wharf

London E14 5HS

Switchboard: 020 7066 1000

Consumer Helpline: 0845 606 1234

Website: www.fsa.gov.uk

Regulates most investments and financial service providers.

Financial Services Compensation Scheme (FSCS)

7th Floor

Lloyds Chambers

Portsoken Street

London E1 8BN

Tel: 020 7892 7300

Website: www.fscs.org.uk

Pays compensation to customers of a financial services company which goes out of business.

Home Improvement Trust

7 Mansfield Road

Nottingham NG1 3FB

Tel: 0115 934 9511

Freephone: 0800 783 7569

Website: www.hitrust.org

May be able to help if you want to release equity to pay for repairs, improvements or adaptations.

IFA Promotion Ltd (IFAP)

2nd Floor

117 Farringdon Road

London EC1R 3BX

Tel: 020 7833 3131

Hotline: 0800 085 3250

Website: www.unbiased.co.uk

Phone the hotline for a list of independent financial advisers in your home or work area.

Institute of Chartered Accountants in England and Wales

Chartered Accountants' Hall

PO Box 433

London EC2P 2BJ

Tel: 020 7920 8100

Scotland: 0131 347 0100

Website: www.icaew.co.uk

For information about choosing and using a chartered accountant.

International Pension Centre

Department for Work and Pensions

Tyneview Park

Whitley Road

Benton

Newcastle upon Tyne NE98 1BA

Tel: 0191 218 7777

For information about pensions and medical cover if you live, or have previously lived, abroad.

Motability

Goodman House

Station Approach

Harlow

Essex CM20 2ET

Tel: 01279 635999

Applications: 0845 456 4566

Website: www.motability.co.uk

For advice and help about cars, scooters and wheelchairs for disabled people.

National Debtline
The Arch
48–52 Floodgate Street
Birmingham B5 5SL
Tel: 0808 808 4000
Website: www.nationaldebtline.co.uk
For advice if you have debt problems.

National Savings & Investments
Blackpool FY3 9YP
Tel: 0845 964 5000
Website: www.nsandi.com
For information about all products from National Savings & Investments.

Pension Schemes Registry
PO Box 1NN
Newcastle upon Tyne NE99 1NN
Tel: 0191 225 6316 (ask for a tracing request form)
Website: www.opra.gov.uk/traceAPension
Will help trace the address of an old pension scheme.

Pensions Advisory Service (OPAS)
11 Belgrave Road
London SW1V 1RB
Helpline: 0845 601 2923
Website: www.opas.org.uk
A voluntary organisation which gives advice and information and helps sort out problems.

Redundancy Payments Office
Customer Service Unit
7th Floor
83–85 Hagley House
Birmingham B16 8QG
Tel: 0845 145 00 04
Website: www.redundancyhelp.co.uk
For information about matters relating to redundancy.

Solicitors Family Law Association
PO Box 302
Orpington
Kent BR6 8QX
Tel: 01689 850227
Website: www.sfla.org.uk
If you need to find a divorce lawyer.

State Pension Forecasting Service
Tel: 0845 3000 168
Website: www.thepensionservice.gov.uk
For a State Pension forecast.

Stock Exchange
Old Broad Street
London EC2N 1HP
Tel: 020 7797 1000
Website: www.londonstockexchange.com
For free booklets and a list of brokers for private investors.

Unclaimed Assets Register (UAR)
Leconfield House
Curzon Street
London W1J 5JA

Tel: 0870 241 1713
Website: www.uar.co.uk
Helps you track down lost money.

Veterans Agency
Norcross
Blackpool FY5 3WP
Tel: 0800 169 22 77
Website: www.veteransagency.mod.uk
For information about War Pensions and all matters of concern to veterans and their families.

USEFUL WEBSITES

www.entitledto.co.uk – is the only one-stop place where you can check your entitlement to tax credits, help with Council Tax and rent, Pension Credit and a wide range of benefits.

www.over50.gov.uk – is a government website where you can find out about work, education, volunteering, health and pensions. You can also download a 78-page booklet which brings together information on all the national and local government services for people over 50.

www.fool.co.uk – The Motley Fool offers down-to-earth information and advice about money (but can seem overwhelmed by adverts).

243

APPENDIX – UPRATING COUNTRIES

There are 25 members of the **European Union (EU)**:

Austria, Belgium, Cyprus, Czech Republic, Denmark, Estonia, Finland, France, Germany, Greece, Hungary, Ireland, Italy, Latvia, Lithuania, Luxembourg, Malta, Netherlands, Poland, Portugal, Slovakia, Slovenia, Spain, Sweden, United Kingdom

There are 28 members of the **European Economic Area (EEA)**:

The 25 members of the EU (as above) plus Iceland, Norway, Liechtenstein

There are 20 other **uprating countries**:

Alderney, Barbados, Bermuda, Bosnia and Herzegovina, Croatia, Federal Republic of Yugoslavia (Serbia), Gibraltar, Guernsey, Isle of Man, Israel, Jamaica, Jersey, Kosovo, Macedonia, Mauritius, Philippines, Sark, Switzerland, Turkey, United States of America. In the Falkland Islands pensions are not uprated by the UK but the local legislative Council tops up frozen UK pensions to the level that would have been paid in the UK.

ABOUT AGE CONCERN

This book is one of a wide range of publications produced by Age Concern England, the National Council on Ageing. Age Concern works on behalf of all older people and believes later life should be fulfilling and enjoyable. For too many this is impossible. As the leading charitable movement in the UK concerned with ageing and older people, Age Concern finds effective ways to change that situation.

Where possible, we enable older people to solve problems themselves, providing as much or as little support as they need. A network of local Age Concerns, supported by many thousands of volunteers, provides community-based services such as lunch clubs, day centres and home visiting.

Nationally, we take a lead role in campaigning, parliamentary work, policy analysis, research, specialist information and advice provision, and publishing. Innovative programmes promote healthier lifestyles and provide older people with opportunities to give the experience of a lifetime back to their communities.

Age Concern is dependent on donations, covenants and legacies.

Age Concern England
1268 London Road
London SW16 4ER
Tel: 020 8765 7200
Fax: 020 8765 7211
Website:
www.ageconcern.org.uk

Age Concern Cymru
4th Floor
1 Cathedral Road
Cardiff CF11 9SD
Tel: 029 2037 1566
Fax: 029 2039 9562
Website: www.accymru.org.uk

Age Concern Scotland
113 Rose Street
Edinburgh EH2 3DT
Tel: 0131 220 3345
Fax: 0131 220 2779
Website:
www.ageconcernscotland.org.uk

Age Concern Northern Ireland
3 Lower Crescent
Belfast BT7 1NR
Tel: 028 9024 5729
Advice line: 028 9032 5055
Fax: 028 9023 5497
Website: www.ageconcernni.org

PUBLICATIONS FROM AGE CONCERN BOOKS

Your Guide to Pensions: Planning Ahead to Boost Retirement Income

Sue Ward

An essential guide for people in their mid-life years who are keen to improve their pension arrangements. It explores, in detail, the main types of pension scheme – State, stakeholder, occupational and personal – and offers guidance on increasing their value. It is updated annually.

Your Taxes and Savings: A Guide for Older People

Paul Lewis

The definitive annual guide to financial planning for older people, this popular book:

- is fully revised and updated
- explains the tax system in clear, concise language
- describes the range of saving and investment options available
- includes model portfolios to illustrate a range of financial scenarios

Your Taxes and Savings explains how the tax system affects people over retirement age, including how to avoid paying more tax than necessary.

Using Your Home as Capital: A Guide to Raising Money from the Value of your Home

Cecil Hinton and Mark Goodale

The best-selling book for homeowners, which is updated annually, gives a detailed explanation of how to capitalise on the value of your home and obtain additional income.

For further information on these three titles please ring 0870 44 22 120.

Changing Direction: Employment Options in Working Life
Sue Ward

Redundancy or early retirement can come as a shock to anybody, but the impact in mid-life can be devastating. This highly practical book is designed to help those aged 40 to 55 get back to work. Always positive and upbeat, it examines issues such as adjusting to change, finances, opportunities for work, deciding what work you really want to do and working for yourself.

£9.99 0-86242-331-7

Retiring to Spain: Everything You Need to Know
Cyril Holbrook

Once free of the shackles of earning a living, thousands of people make the momentous move to head south to the sun. Living in Spain is an entirely different experience from going there on holiday. This book will help people avoid many of the pitfalls, and enable them to make the transition to a sunny and healthy retirement.

£7.99 0-86242-385-6

Your Guide to Retirement
Ro Lyon

A comprehensive handbook for older people on the point of retirement, this book is full of practical information and advice on all the opportunities available. It also points readers in the right direction to obtain more information when required. Drawing on Age Concern's wealth of experience, it covers everything you need to know, including:

- managing your money
- staying healthy
- making the most of your time

- housing options
- relationships

Your Guide to Retirement is easy to use and designed to encourage everyone to view retirement as an opportunity not to be missed. £7.99 0-86242-350-3

If you would like to order any of these titles, please write to the address below, enclosing a cheque or money order for the appropriate amount (plus £1.99 p&p for one book; for additional books please add 75p per book up to a maximum of £7.50) made payable to Age Concern England. Credit card orders may be made on 0870 44 22 120. Books can also be ordered online at www.ageconcern.org.uk/shop

Age Concern Books
Units 5 and 6
Industrial Estate
Brecon
Powys LD3 8LA

Bulk order discounts

Age Concern Books is pleased to offer a discount on orders totalling 50 or more copies of the same title. For details, please contact Age Concern Books on 0870 44 22 120.

Customised editions

Age Concern Books is pleased to offer a free 'customisation' service for anyone wishing to purchase 500 or more copies of the same title. This gives you the option to have a unique front cover design featuring your organisation's logo and corporate colours, or adding your logo to the current cover design. You can also insert an additional four pages of text for a small additional fee. Existing clients include many of the biggest names in British industry, retailing and finance, the trades unions, educational establishments, the statutory and voluntary sectors, and welfare associations. For full details, please contact Sue Henning, Age Concern Books, Astral House, 1268 London Road, London SW16 4ER. Tel: 020 8765 7200. Fax: 020 8765 7211. Email: hennins@ace.org.uk

Visit our website at: www.ageconcern.org.uk/shop

AGE CONCERN INFORMATION LINE/ FACTSHEETS SUBSCRIPTION

Age Concern produces more than 45 comprehensive factsheets designed to answer many of the questions older people (or those advising them) may have. These include money and benefits, health, community care, leisure and education, and housing. For up to five free factsheets, telephone 0800 00 99 66 (7am–7pm, seven days a week, every day of the year). Alternatively you may prefer to write to Age Concern, Freepost (SWB 30375), ASHBURTON, Devon TQ13 7ZZ.

For professionals working with older people, the factsheets are available on an annual subscription service, which includes updates throughout the year. For further details and costs of the subscription, please contact Age Concern at the above address.

INDEX

We hope that this publication has been useful to you. If so, we would very much like to hear from you. Alternatively, if you feel that we could add or change anything, then please write and tell us, using the following Freepost address: Age Concern, FREEPOST CN1794, London SW16 4BR.